TALKING BODIES

The John Bowlby Memorial Conference Monographs Series

Other titles in this series:

Touch: Attachment and the Body
edited by Kate White

Unmasking Race, Culture, and Attachment in the Psychoanalytic Space
edited by Kate White

Sexuality and Attachment in Clinical Practice
edited by Kate White and Joseph Schwartz

Trauma and Attachment
edited by Sarah Benamer and Kate White

Shattered States: Disorganized Attachment and Its Repair
edited by Judy Yellin and Kate White

Terror Within and Without: Attachment and Disintegration: Clinical Work on the Edge
edited by Judy Yellin and Orit Badouk Epstein

TALKING BODIES
How Do We Integrate Working with the Body in Psychotherapy from an Attachment and Relational Perspective?

THE JOHN BOWLBY MEMORIAL
CONFERENCE MONOGRAPH 2012

Edited by
Kate White

The John Bowlby Memorial Conference Monographs
Series Editor: Kate White

KARNAC

First published in 2014 by
Karnac Books Ltd
118 Finchley Road
London NW3 5HT

Copyright © 2014 to Kate White for the edited collection, and to the individual authors for their contributions.

The rights of the contributors to be identified as the authors of this work have been asserted in accordance with §§ 77 and 78 of the Copyright Design and Patents Act 1988.

All rights reserved. No part of this publication may be reproduced, stored in a retrieval system, or transmitted, in any form or by any means, electronic, mechanical, photocopying, recording, or otherwise, without the prior written permission of the publisher.

British Library Cataloguing in Publication Data

A C.I.P. for this book is available from the British Library

ISBN-13: 978-1-78220-106-9

Typeset by V Publishing Solutions Pvt Ltd., Chennai, India

www.karnacbooks.com

CONTENTS

ACKNOWLEDGEMENTS vii

ABOUT THE EDITOR AND CONTRIBUTORS ix

INTRODUCTION xiii
Kate White

CHAPTER ONE
Attachment theory and the John Bowlby Memorial
  Lecture 2012: a short history 1
Kate White

CHAPTER TWO
Four relational modes of attending to the body
  in psychotherapy 11
Roz Carroll

CHAPTER THREE
Embodiment and the social bond 41
Nick Totton

CHAPTER FOUR
Attachment and energy psychology: explorations at the interface of bodily, mental, relational, and transpersonal aspects of human behaviour and experience   65
Phil Mollon

CHAPTER FIVE
Wisdom of the body, lost and found: the nineteenth John Bowlby Memorial Lecture   89
Pat Ogden

CHAPTER SIX
Touching trauma: working relationally and safely with the unboundaried body   109
Orit Badouk Epstein

CHAPTER SEVEN
The body I want: a psychotherapy with a disabled man   125
Mark Linington

APPENDIX ONE
Recommended reading   143

APPENDIX TWO
The Bowlby Centre   147

INDEX   150

ACKNOWLEDGEMENTS

Thanks to the members of the John Bowlby Memorial Conference 2012 Planning Group: Orit Badouk Epstein, France Couelle, Helene Everitt, Brenda Prince and Judy Yellin for their creative work in producing yet another stimulating and groundbreaking conference that has enabled the emergence of this important publication. Also, many thanks to all the contributors to the conference, whose profound, creative and courageous work can now reach a much wider audience.

Particular thanks to our nineteenth John Bowlby Memorial Lecturer 2012, Dr Pat Ogden, whose innovative presentation provided a context for the leading-edge clinical discussions emerging out of this conference.

A special thank you to Oliver Rathbone for his continuing belief in the value of publishing these monographs, and to his colleagues at Karnac Books for their patience and support in their production and publication.

Kate White,
Editor and Series Editor,
John Bowlby Memorial Conference Monographs

ABOUT THE EDITOR AND CONTRIBUTORS

Orit Badouk Epstein is an attachment-based psychoanalytic psychotherapist (UKCP registered) and a supervisor working in private practice. She works relationally with all client groups and has a particular interest and passion for working with individuals who have experienced extreme abuse and trauma, displaying symptoms of dissociation. Orit is a trustee of the Clinic for Dissociative Studies. She is co-author of *Ritual Abuse and Mind Control: The Manipulation of Attachment Needs* (Karnac). She regularly writes articles and film and book reviews and is Associate Editor of the journal *Attachment: New Directions in Psychotherapy & Relational Psychoanalysis* and the ESTD newsletter.

Roz Carroll is a Chiron-trained body psychotherapist. Over the past two decades she has vigorously pursued interdisciplinary dialogue, and counts relational psychoanalysis, attachment theory, authentic movement and neuroscience as some of the most important influences on her work. Roz teaches at The Minster Centre and Terapia, and has given many lectures for Confer. She is the author of numerous articles and chapters including, most recently, *Self-Regulation—An Evolving Concept at the Heart of Body Psychotherapy* in *Contemporary Body Psychotherapy* edited by Linda Hartley and published by Routledge in 2009. She has a website at www.thinkbody.co.uk.

Mark Linington is an attachment-based psychoanalytic psychotherapist. He trained at The Bowlby Centre, where he is a training supervisor and teacher. He has worked for more than ten years in the NHS as a psychotherapist with people with learning disabilities who have been traumatised. He has a private practice including work with young people with special needs.

Phil Mollon, PhD, is a psychoanalyst and psychotherapist with a background profession of clinical psychology. He has written widely on the impact of trauma on human development, and has drawn particularly upon the "self psychology" of Heinz Kohut. Always searching for more effective ways of helping those who have suffered trauma, he explored psychoanalytic perspectives on EMDR, and for the last thirteen years has been immersed in the study of "energy psychology", a genre of gentle yet highly effective techniques that work concurrently with the mind and the body's subtle energy system. He is the author of ten books, his most recent being *Psychoanalytic Energy Psychotherapy* (2008). Dr Mollon has worked within the NHS for over forty years.

Pat Ogden, PhD, is the founder and director of the Sensorimotor Psychotherapy Institute, an internationally recognised school that specialises in training psychotherapists in somatic/cognitive approaches for the treatment of trauma, developmental and attachment issues. She is a co-founder of the Hakomi Institute, has been a faculty member of The Naropa University since 1985, and lectures internationally. A pioneer in somatic psychotherapy and the treatment of trauma, Dr Ogden is trained in a wide variety of somatic and psychotherapeutic approaches and has over forty years of experience working with individuals and groups. She is the first author of the groundbreaking book *Trauma and the Body: A Sensorimotor Approach to Psychotherapy*, which was published in the autumn of 2006 in the interpersonal neurobiology series of W. W. Norton, and is currently working on her second book, *The Body as Resource: Sensorimotor Interventions for the Treatment of Trauma*.

Nick Totton is a therapist and trainer with nearly thirty years' experience. Originally a Reichian body therapist, his approach has become broad-based and open to the spontaneous and unexpected. Nick has an MA in Psychoanalytic Studies, and has worked with process-oriented psychology and trained as a craniosacral therapist. He is currently involved with ecopsychology and addressing climate change, and is chair of Psychotherapists and Counsellors for Social Responsibility. He has a twenty-five year old daughter. Nick has written or edited several books, including *Psychotherapy and Politics* (2000); *Body Psychotherapy: An Introduction* (2003); *Press When Illuminated: New and Selected Poems* (2004); and, most recently, *Wild Therapy* (2011) published by PCCS Books. See www.erthworks.co.uk. He lives in Calderdale with his partner, and grows vegetables.

Kate White is a training therapist, supervisor and teacher at The Bowlby Centre, and the acting editor of *Attachment: New Directions in Psychotherapy and Relational Psychoanalysis*. Formerly a senior lecturer at South Bank University, London, in the Department of Nursing and Community Health Studies, she has used her extensive experience in adult education to contribute to the innovative psychotherapy curriculum developed at The Bowlby Centre. In addition to working as an individual psychotherapist, Kate writes about psychotherapy education and runs workshops on the themes of attachment and trauma in clinical practice. Informed by her experience of growing up in South Africa, she has long been interested in the impact of race and culture on theory and on clinical practice.

INTRODUCTION

Kate White

As I sit down to write this introduction to the nineteenth John Bowlby Memorial Conference 2012 on the theme of "Talking Bodies: How do we Integrate Working with the Body in Psychotherapy from an Attachment and Relational Perspective?" I am reminded that it was ten years ago that I was involved in the planning of the tenth conference in this series entitled "Touch: Attachment and the Body", where Susie Orbach delivered the John Bowlby Memorial Lecture with the title "The Body in Clinical Practice". In this groundbreaking event, the under-theorising of the body within psychoanalytic psychotherapy at that time was highlighted.

> Perhaps relational approaches to psychoanalytic psychotherapy have underplayed the central role of the body in constructing experience and the shaping of our internal worlds. The child's longing for the body of the mother has always been implicit in Attachment theory. Yet perhaps in reaction to the excesses of certain classical theories, and because of its need to achieve scientific respectability, the body and by implication touch, the sexual and the erotic have been under theorised. (White, 2004, p. xxiv)

At the same event Colwyn Trevarthen, the renowned developmental psychologist, is quoted as saying:

> I am sure therapists need a model of non-verbal communication based upon acceptance of intrinsic affective states and their communication by active contact between bodies in all degrees of intimacy. (Trevarthen, 2004, p. 11)

In Susie Orbach's lecture of that year (2003) she reminds us that "mindedness to the body as a body which is speaking for itself and its difficulties is peculiarly absent" (Orbach, 2004, p. 21).

She continues:

> Our body like our psychic properties and potentialities, emerges out of the emotional ambience and bodily interaction with our caregivers. Our personal body unfolds and develops its individuality in the context of its relationship to and with an other and other bodies. (Orbach, 2004, p. 23)

Taking into account the significance of body countertransference in our work, Susie Orbach discussed her re-evaluation of the reading of bodily symptoms as representing "the struggle of the body to come to therapy and to come into being" (Orbach, 2004, p. 24) in addition to the more commonly held view that "symptoms" were communicating a state of mind. Her argument continued, asserting that "The body is only made in relationship" and in a paraphrase of Winnicott's "there is no such thing as a baby" her suggestion is that there is "no such thing as a body, there is only a body in relationship with another body" (Orbach, 2004, p. 28). Her lecture concluded with identifying the need for us to re-theorise the relationship between body and mind and its impact on practice (Orbach, 2004, p. 33).

Nine years on, and the 2012 conference can be seen as a reflection of how we have, at The Bowlby Centre, continued to be at the forefront of that exploration called for back in 2003, with remarkable and radical contributions from two of our members, Mark Linington and Orit Badouk Epstein. Each in their different ways have brought their clinical experiences to life in their presentations, and demonstrated this leading-edge work in relation to the themes of the body and touch with clients so often regarded as "unsuitable for therapy", namely those who have a physical or learning disability or those who have survived extreme trauma through the painful means of psychic protection, resulting in dissociative states of mind.

The aim of this conference was to explore the growing role of the body in the context of relational psychoanalysis and psychotherapy over the last decade, and bring us up to date in thinking about the relationship between attachment, the body, and trauma. Questions addressed included: How do we anchor the new understandings we are gaining within the framework of attachment? How might the integration of these ideas about the body change what we do in the consulting room? What impact might this have on the therapy relationship? Can we maintain and respect the place of a secure, attuned attachment between therapist and client, and its healing potential, at the centre of our therapeutic work?

It is notable that in this conference, through the developments in attachment theory in clinical practice and the relational approach to therapeutic work, there was a greater integration between therapists who come from a body-oriented psychotherapy tradition and those who have been trained in a relational and psychodynamic tradition.

This sense of emerging integration was the inspiration behind the invitation to Pat Ogden, an eminent body-oriented psychotherapist, to give the nineteenth John Bowlby Memorial Lecture. She has, with her colleagues, pioneered sensorimotor psychotherapy, which uses a combination of somatic and cognitive approaches in work with people who have experienced trauma, developmental difficulties, and insecure attachment relationships. Her chapter entitled "Wisdom of the body, lost and found" was a tour de force in which she, with characteristic energy and enthusiasm, delighted the audience with a wonderful exploration of these issues within the context of her delicate work with clients. She showed us both visually through videotape and in her spoken word how her engagement both emotionally and bodily with her clients had profound and moving impact, bringing people into a more embodied and comfortable relationally attuned place with the other and within their bodies. Her discussion of the role of self-states and the complexity of working models in this work are illuminating of clinical practice. Similarly her unpacking of the experience of proximity-seeking behaviour in clients and ourselves—and how understanding it from an attachment theory perspective gives us a range of empathic responses—was amply illustrated in her moving account of her therapeutic relationship with Simon. Her conference presentation has translated into a beautifully articulated chapter taking our thinking to a new level of understanding.

The presentations leading up to the main lecture provided a textured and in-depth background context to the theme of "Talking Bodies". The opening address was given by Roz Carroll, an experienced and articulate body psychotherapist, who over the last two decades has vigorously pursued interdisciplinary dialogue, and counts relational psychoanalysis, attachment theory, authentic movement and neuroscience as some of the most important influences on her work. Her presentation was entitled "Four relational modes of attending to the body in psychotherapy". Commenting on the sea change in the recognition of the centrality of the body in our field and its links to all that makes us human, she says "… brain and body, self and other, nervous system and environment, influence and respond to each other, 'riffing' off each other as jazz musicians do" (Carroll, 2013, p. 12, this volume).

Roz deftly weaves a framework from Stephen Mitchell's four "modes" of relating described in his book *Relationality: From Attachment to Intersubjectivity* (2000). These she describes as "differentiated aspects of therapeutic work that are applicable to all relational psychotherapies, and indeed all creative human relationships." These different "lenses" are: non-reflective behaviour, affect permeability, self–other configuration, and intersubjectivity, and can be used to deepen our understanding and development of an embodied engagement with our clients and each other. It is a two-person process in which the therapist's body is as significant to understand and read as the client's in their mutual encounter. She uses an extended and beautifully nuanced account of her clinical work to illustrate this way of working and understanding human, embodied, relational, psychotherapeutic encounters.

Nick Totton's contribution focuses on the practice and theory of body psychotherapy itself, developing a grounded understanding of what the often-used phrase "embodied relationship" really involves. He looks at the clinical implications and suggests how we can move beyond the infant-focused concept of "attachment" to think instead about the nature of our social bond and our bond with the other-than-human in a lively and discursive chapter.

In the last decade, there has been an explosion of therapeutic interest in the role of the body in holding traumatic feeling states in the form of "body memories". Insights from work with clients increasingly demonstrate that, as leading traumatologist Bessel van der Kolk puts it, "the body keeps the score". Whether clients have experienced the "big T" trauma of a major event or the cumulative relational trauma born of a history of insecure attachments and complex post-traumatic stress disorder (PTSD), patterns of emotional distress become encoded physically. Trauma remains "locked" in the body, potentially disrupting and blocking the effective healing of traumatic relational injuries within the therapeutic relationship.

The field is evolving fast, with rapidly developing contributions from neuroscience, sensorimotor therapies, eye movement desensitisation and reprocessing (EMDR), and other new techniques, offering fresh ways of helping clients regulate the emotional legacy of trauma, extending the tools of psychotherapy beyond speech. Whilst these new approaches are generating considerable interest among clinicians, many therapists remain uncertain about whether and how we can use them with our own clients within primarily talking therapies.

It is in this context that the chapter by Phil Mollon extends our knowledge and understanding of the use of "energy psychology", which is particularly helpful. "Attachment and energy psychology: explorations at the interface of bodily, mental, relational, and transpersonal aspects of human behaviour and experience" was the title of his presentation. He gives a clear and succinct account of this approach, and a clinical example of how this works within a thoughtful and ethical clinical practice. He is very careful to point out that what he advocates is a very particular and unique integration of approaches known as Psychoanalytic Energy Psychotherapy (PEP) the practice of which, in addition to specifics of PEP, requires a background training and the prior experience gained as a psychoanalytic psychotherapist.

Our final two chapters have been written by experienced clinicians from The Bowlby Centre. "The body I want: a psychotherapy with a disabled man" by Mark Linington and "Touching trauma: working relationally and safely with the unboundaried body" by Orit Badouk Epstein.

Mark Linington's chapter brings an extraordinary contribution to our understanding of the particular additional struggle people with a physical or learning disability have in finding a place to confidently inhabit their bodies–bodies that have often been shunned, despised, unwelcomed and hated from birth. Mark's in-depth account of his work illuminates the agonising pain of difference as it relates to corporeality, as he says—it is often the case that in working with someone from a marginalised and ostracised group, issues that can remain hidden but which affect us all can be more clearly understood. He explores with openness the complexity and challenges from an attachment perspective of establishing a co-created, two-bodied, intersubjective and healing relationship with someone with a deeply traumatised body.

Orit Badouk Epstein has developed a unique understanding of the different types of touch and their use in therapeutic work. Her understanding is informed by attachment theory and the extensive research in the world of post-traumatic stress on bodily states and our universal need for safe bodily responses to affect dysregulated states. She provides an important overview of how the use of touch has become so distrusted within a psychodynamic approach to therapy, and makes a cogent case for its benefits within a boundaried and thought through attachment-based and relationally informed psychotherapy.

On the morning of the conference I had just received a copy of the last known interview with John Bowlby (Hunter, 1990), and it was with great interest I read his answer to Virginia Hunter's question.

> VH: We see so many adults and children now, or I do, that may be functioning very well and yet they feel like they don't have a container around them. They feel like they don't have a skin. And I'm thinking, now, about the concept of "the body near mother." With children … we usually … hug them or pat them or make contact with their skin. In psychoanalysis there's a taboo on any physical contact. My own experience … is that there are times when a gentle touch does seem to contain them or help make some feeling connection to them that they might not be able to make otherwise.

Bowlby in his reply agrees that this is a "hot potato" as in his words

> touch can so easily mean sex … They're not inevitably connected … I think that the truth of the matter is, that in therapeutic work touch can, in certain circumstances between two people be very valuable and therapeutic, but it also has to be used with quite a lot of discretion …
>
> As a male therapist one has to be careful about using touch, but that doesn't mean to say I haven't used touch, because I have.

... I helped a widow in a very distressed position, grieving for her husband, and I put my arms around her, and I let her cry on my knee. So I'm not averse to it, but you need to stay in control.

VH: It's such an important subject, I think, because people seem almost phobic to discuss it.

JB: Sure it's something which is both very important and full of pitfalls. It's a difficult subject to do systematic research on for the reasons we have discussed, and there is very little systematic research in point of fact and that's a pity. (Hunter, 1990, pp. 16–18)

Following on from these observations of Bowlby's it is so important that we share our clinical experience in this area so as to build on good practice and add to the clinical research already available. There are enormous developments within the field of neuroscience where the understanding of how our bodies are "talking" and communicating is confirming much of what we know and understand from our countertransference in clinical practice. Hence the desirability of a conference like this where we can bring our experience together and discuss it from different perspectives in order to learn from one another as well as those with whom we work. It also challenges us to question ourselves and be open to new developments and approaches. These discussions brought to a conclusion an extraordinarily thought-provoking set of presentations—each contributor bringing their thoughts and feelings and breadth of experience to share with us and extend the field in a profoundly radical way.

References

Hunter, V. (1990). John Bowlby: An Interview. Transcript in Tavistock Clinic Library.

Orbach, S. (2004). The body in clinical practice, part one: There's no such thing as a body. In: K. White (Ed.), *Touch: Attachment and the Body* (pp. 17–34). London: Karnac.

Orbach, S. (2004). The body in clinical practice, part two: When touch comes to therapy. In: K. White (Ed.), *Touch: Attachment and the Body* (pp. 35–47). London: Karnac.

Trevarthen, C. (2004). Intimate contact from birth. In: K. White (Ed.), *Touch: Attachment and the Body* (pp. 1–15). London: Karnac.

White, K. (Ed.) (2004). *Touch: Attachment and the Body*. London: Karnac.

CHAPTER ONE

Attachment theory and the John Bowlby Memorial Lecture 2012: a short history

Kate White

(Based on an original article by Bernice Laschinger)

This year marks nineteen years since the first John Bowlby Memorial Lecture was given by Colin Murray Parkes on the theme of mourning and loss. That was a fitting recognition of Bowlby's great contribution to the understanding of human grief and sadness, while his clinical observations of separation and loss laid down the foundations of attachment theory. This year's lecturer is Pat Ogden, a pioneer in the field of somatic psychology and the founder/director of the Sensorimotor Psychotherapy Institute, an internationally recognised school specialising in somatic-cognitive approaches for the treatment of post-traumatic stress and attachment disturbances.

In the years which have followed that first conference, attachment theory, in the words of Cassidy and Shaver (2008, p. xi), has produced "one of the broadest, most profound and most creative lines of research in 20th-century (and now 21st-century) psychology". Nevertheless, given the hostility of the psychoanalytic establishment to Bowlby's ideas, it has only been in the last two decades, during which there have been dramatic advances in the congruent disciplines of infancy research

1

and relational psychoanalysis, that the clinical relevance of attachment theory has been unquestionably established.

Indeed, it has been the development of its clinical applications—in tandem with its evolving convergence with psychoanalysis and trauma theory—that has been central to our practice at The Bowlby Centre. Looking back, our very early links with Bowlby's work were forged by one of our founders John Southgate, who had clinical supervision with John Bowlby. Bowlby's understanding of the nature of human relatedness became primary in our theoretical framework and practice. It contributed directly to our emergence as an attachment-based psychoanalytic centre in 1992.

In 2007 the John Bowlby Memorial Conference marked the centenary of John Bowlby's birth in 1907. One of the outstanding psychoanalysts of the twentieth century, as a theory builder and reformer, his societal impact and influence on social policy have been greater than that of any other. He has been described by Diana Diamond as "the Dickens of psychoanalytic theory": he illuminated the human experiences of attachment and loss as vividly as Dickens represented those of poverty and deprivation.

The origins of Bowlby's work lay in his early work with children displaced through war or institutionalisation. This led him to the conviction that at the heart of traumatic experience lay parental loss and prolonged separation from parents. His landmark report for the World Health Organization, *Maternal Care and Mental Health*, enabled him to establish definitively the primary link between environmental trauma and the disturbed development of children (1952).

With these understandings, he entered the public arena to bring about change in the way childhood suffering was addressed by the adult world. Bowlby's work created a bridge over the chasm between individual and social experience, and hence between the personal and the political.

There is congruence between the social and therapeutic perspectives of John Bowlby and those of the John Bowlby Memorial Lecturer in 2008 Judith Herman, author of *Father Daughter Incest* (2000) and *Trauma and Recovery* (1992). She, too, has directed her life's work to the "restoring of connections" between the private and public worlds in which traumatic experience takes place; but her focus has been on the traumatic experiences that take place in adulthood. She has shown the parallels between private terrors such as rape and domestic violence, and public traumas such as political terrorism. Her conceptual framework for psychotherapy with traumatised people points to the major importance of attachment in the empowerment of the survivor. She writes: "Recovery can take place only within the context of relationships; it cannot occur in isolation" (1992, p. 133).

Bowlby had also sought to bridge the chasm between clinician and researcher. His preparedness to leave the closed world of psychoanalysis of his time in order to make links with other disciplines such as animal studies and academic psychology was vital in the building up of attachment theory. The documented and filmed sequence of children's responses to separation in terms of protest, detachment, and despair, as researched by James Robertson, provided evidence of separation anxiety. The impact of these ideas on the development of care of children in hospital has been enormous. The 2001 John Bowlby Memorial Lecturer, Michael Rutter, discussed institutional care and the role of the state in promoting recovery from neglect and abuse. His lecture was a testament to the continuing relevance of Bowlby's thinking to contemporary social issues.

Although Bowlby joined the British Psychoanalytical Society in the 1930s and received his training from Joan Riviere and Melanie Klein, he became increasingly sceptical of their focus on the inner fantasy life of the child rather than real life experience, and tended towards what would now be termed a relational approach. Thus, in searching for a theory that could explain the anger and distress of separated young children, Bowlby turned to disciplines outside psychoanalysis such as ethology. He became convinced of the relevance of animal, and particularly primate, behaviour to our understanding of the normal process of attachment. These relational concepts presented a serious challenge to the closed world of psychoanalysis in the 1940s, and earned Bowlby the hostility of his erstwhile colleagues for several decades.

The maintenance of physical proximity by a young animal to a preferred adult is found in a number of animal species. This suggested to Bowlby that attachment behaviour has a survival value, the most likely function of which is that of care and protection, particularly from predators. It is activated by conditions such as sickness, fear, and fatigue. Threat of loss leads to anxiety and anger; actual loss leads to anger and sorrow. When efforts to restore the bond fail, attachment behaviour may diminish, but will persist at an unconscious level and may become reactivated by reminders of the lost adult, or new experiences of loss.

Attachment theory's basic premise is that, from the beginning of life, the baby human has a primary need to establish an emotional bond with a caregiving adult. Attachment is seen as a source of human motivation as fundamental as those of food and sex. Bowlby (1979, p. 129) postulated that "Attachment behaviour is any form of behaviour that results in a person attaining or maintaining proximity to some other preferred and differentiated individual ... While especially evident during early childhood, attachment behaviour is held to characterise human beings from the cradle to the grave."

Attachment theory highlights the importance of mourning in relation to trauma and loss. An understanding of the relevance of this to therapeutic practice was a vital element in the foundation of The Bowlby Centre. The consequences of disturbed and unresolved mourning processes was a theme taken up by Colin Murray Parkes when he gave the first John Bowlby Memorial Lecture in 1993.

Mary Ainsworth, an American psychologist who became Bowlby's lifelong collaborator, established the interconnectedness between attachment behaviour, caregiving in the adult, and exploration in the child. While the child's need to explore and the need for proximity might seem contradictory, they are in fact complementary. It is the mother's provision of a secure base, to which the child can return after exploration, which enables the development of self-reliance and autonomy. Ainsworth developed the Strange Situation Procedure for studying individual differences in the attachment patterns of young children. She was able to correlate these to their mother's availability and responsiveness. Her work provided both attachment theory and psychoanalysis with empirical support for some basic premises. This provided the necessary link between attachment concepts and their application to individual experience in a clinical setting.

Over the last two decades the perspective of attachment theory has been greatly extended by the work of Mary Main, who was another John Bowlby Memorial Lecturer. She developed the Adult Attachment Interview in order to study the unconscious processes that underlie the behavioural pattern of attachment identified by Mary Ainsworth. Further support came from the perspective of infant observation and developmental psychology developed by yet another John Bowlby Memorial Lecturer, Daniel Stern. The John Bowlby Memorial Lecturer for 2000, Allan Schore, presented important developments in the new field of neuro-psychoanalysis, describing emerging theories of how attachment experiences in early life shape the developing brain.

The links between attachment theory and psychoanalysis have also been developed. Jo Klein, a great supporter of The Bowlby Centre and also a former contributor to the John Bowlby Memorial Conference, has explored these links in psychotherapeutic practice. In particular, the 1998 Bowlby Lecturer, the late Stephen Mitchell, identified a paradigm shift away from drive theory within psychoanalysis. His proposed "relational matrix" links attachment theory to other relational psychoanalytic theories, which find so much resonance in the current social and cultural climate. Within this area of convergence, between attachment research and developmental psychoanalysis, the 1999 John Bowlby Memorial Lecturer Peter Fonagy has developed the concept of "mentalization", extending our understanding of the importance of the reflective function, particularly in adversity.

In a similar vein, the work of Beatrice Beebe, the 2001 John Bowlby Memorial Lecturer, represents another highly creative development in the unfolding relational narrative of the researcher-clinician dialogue. Her unique research has demonstrated how the parent–infant interaction creates a distinct system organised by mutual influence and regulation, which is reproduced in the adult therapeutic relationship.

In the movement to bring the body into the forefront of relational theory and practice, the 2003 John Bowlby Memorial Lecturer Susie Orbach has been a leading pioneer. It was the publication of her groundbreaking books, *Fat is a Feminist Issue* (1978) and *Hunger Strike* (1986) that introduced a powerful and influential approach to the study of the body in its social context. Over the last decade, one of her major interests has been the construction of sexuality and bodily experience in the therapeutic relationship.

The 2004 John Bowlby Memorial Lecturer Jody Messler Davies has made major contributions to the development of the relational model. Her integration of trauma theory and relational psychoanalysis led to new understandings of the transference-countertransference as a vehicle for expressing traumatic experience (Davies & Frawley, 1994).

Kimberlyn Leary, our John Bowlby Memorial Lecturer in 2005, illuminated the impact of racism on the clinical process. The importance of her contribution lay in her understanding of the transformative potential inherent in the collision of two "racialised subjectivities" in the therapeutic process. She showed the possibility for reparation when both therapist and client break the silence surrounding their difference.

The contribution of the 2006 John Bowlby Memorial Lecturer Bessel van der Kolk to the understanding of post-traumatic stress as a developmental trauma disorder has been seminal (2005). His book *Psychological Trauma* was the first to consider the impact of trauma on the entire person, integrating neurobiological, interpersonal and social perspectives (1987).

Within this tradition of great trauma theorists, the contribution of John Bowlby Memorial Lecturer 2007 Judith Herman, a collaborator of Bessel van der Kolk, has been outstanding. As a teacher, researcher, and clinician, her life's work has been directed to survivors of trauma. Her landmark book *Trauma and Recovery* (1992) is considered to have changed the way we think about trauma. Bridging the world of war veterans, prisoners of war, and survivors of domestic and sexual abuse, she has shown that psychological trauma can only be understood in a social context.

In 2008 our John Bowlby Memorial Lecturer was Arietta Slade, a widely published clinician, researcher, and teacher. Her work has been enormously significant in the movement to link attachment theory with clinical ideas (1999b, 2008). She has pioneered attachment-based approaches to clinical work with both adults and children, including the development of parental reflective functioning and the relational contexts of play and early symbolisation. There is also a congruence between her current work and the spirit of Bowlby's early clinical observations. She has shifted the therapeutic focus away from the formal categorisation of attachment patterns, to questions about how the attachment system functions to regulate fear and distress within the therapeutic process, significantly where there are "dynamic disruptions".

Arietta Slade's work represents a highly significant development in the application of attachment theory to clinical work (1999a). Following on the work of Main (1994) and Fonagy (1999) she has demonstrated how an attachment-based understanding of the development of representation and affect regulation in the child and his or her mother offers us potentially transformative insights into the nature of the therapeutic process and change.

In 2009 we were honoured to welcome Amanda Jones to give the John Bowlby Memorial Lecture. She presented her work with troubled parents and their children—highlighted in the television series

Help Me Love My Baby. Her work has been acclaimed for its capacity to demonstrate the effectiveness of interventions where the parent is offered a long-term compassionate attachment relationship in which their own story of trauma is shared. This provides a possibility for reflectiveness and intergenerational change.

Our John Bowlby Memorial Lecturer in 2010 was Jude Cassidy, a pioneer in the attachment tradition of research with clinical applications. She was a student of Bowlby's primary collaborator Mary Ainsworth and has extended attachment theory's reach in both the fields of childhood and adolescence. As an author and editor she has had a prominent role in the publication of attachment theory, research findings and their clinical application. Jude Cassidy is Professor of Psychology at the University of Maryland, and director of the Maryland Child and Family Development Laboratory. She received her PhD in 1986 from the University of Virginia where her mentor was Mary Ainsworth. Jude Cassidy's research includes a focus on early intervention. Her concerns are wide ranging, focusing on attachment, social and emotional development in children and adolescents, social information-processing, peer relations, and longitudinal prediction of adolescent risk behaviour. These were all areas that were pertinent to our theme in 2009 of "Attachment in the 21st Century; Where Next?"

In 2012 the John Bowlby Memorial Lecturer was Dr Sandra L. Bloom, who has a long association with The Bowlby Centre as she has been our consultant on trauma for many years. Sandy Bloom is a psychiatrist, currently Associate Professor of Health Management and Policy and Co-Director of the Center for Nonviolence and Social Justice at the School of Public Health of Drexel University in Philadelphia. She is best known to us through her imaginative and pioneering work for twenty-one years as director of The Sanctuary Programmes, an inpatient mental health intervention for adults maltreated as children. Here she developed a humane and compassionate centre caring for those traumatised in early life, using the work of John Bowlby as its central conceptual framework. An account of this work is to be found in her publications, Bloom (2013) and Bloom and Farragher, (2010, 2013).

This year we welcome Pat Ogden to deliver the nineteenth John Bowlby Memorial Lecture on the theme of the links between attachment, trauma, and the body. Her work uses a variety of approaches that focus on the physical as well as the psychological aspects of trauma, providing an integration that she has written about with colleagues in their book *Trauma and the Body: A Sensorimotor Approach to Psychotherapy* (Ogden, Minton & Pain, 2006). Her work is informed by contemporary research in neuroscience, attachment theory, trauma, and related fields.

References

Bloom, S. L. (2013). *Creating Sanctuary: Toward the Evolution of Sane Societies* (2nd edn). New York: Routledge.
Bloom, S. L., & Farragher, B. (2010). *Destroying Sanctuary: The Crisis in Human Service Delivery Systems*. New York: Oxford University Press.
Bloom, S. L., & Farragher, B. (2013). *Restoring Sanctuary: A New Operating System for Trauma-Informed Systems of Care*. New York: Oxford University Press.
Bowlby, J. (1952). *Maternal Care and Mental Health* (2nd edn). [World Health Organization: Monograph Series, No. 2.] Geneva, Switzerland: World Health Organization.
Bowlby, J. (1979). *The Making and Breaking of Affectional Bonds*. London: Tavistock.
Cassidy, J., & Shaver, P. (2008). *Handbook of Attachment: Theory, Research and Clinical Applications*. New York: Guilford Press.
Davies, J. M., & Frawley, M. G. (1994). *Treating the Adult Survivor of Childhood Sexual Abuse: A Psychoanalytic Perspective*. New York: Basic.
Fonagy, P. (1999). Psychoanalytic theory from the point of view of attachment theory and research. In: J. Cassidy & P. R. Shaver (Eds.), *Handbook of Attachment Theory and Research*. New York: Guilford Press.
Herman, J. L. (1992). *Trauma and Recovery: The Aftermath of Violence from Domestic Abuse to Political Terror*. New York: Basic.
Herman, J. L. (2000). *Father Daughter Incest*. Cambridge, MA: Harvard University Press.
Main, M. (1994). A move to the level of representation in the study of attachment organization: Implications for psychoanalysis. *Bulletin of the British Psycho-Analytical Society*, 1–15.
Ogden, P., Pain, C., & Minton, K. (2006). *Trauma and the Body: A Sensorimotor Approach to Psychotherapy*. New York: Norton.
Orbach, S. (1978). *Fat is a Feminist Issue*. London: Paddington Press.
Orbach, S. (1986). *Hunger Strike: The Anorectic's Struggle as a Metaphor for Our Time*. London: Faber and Faber.
Slade, A. (1999a). Representation, symbolization and affect regulation. *Psychoanalytic Inquiry, 19*: 797–830.

Slade, A. (1999b). Attachment theory and research. In: *Handbook of Attachment: Theory, Research and Clinical Applications* (pp. 575–591). New York: Guilford Press.

Slade, A. (2008). The move from categories to process: Attachment phenomena and clinical evaluation in attachment. *New Directions in Psychotherapy and Relational Psychoanalysis, 2*(1): 89–105.

Van der Kolk, B. (1987). *Psychological Trauma*. Washington, DC: American Psychiatric Press.

Van der Kolk, B. (2005). Developmental trauma disorder. *Psychiatric Annals, 35*(5): 401–408.

CHAPTER TWO

Four relational modes of attending to the body in psychotherapy

Roz Carroll

What do we mean by the body?

For some in the field of psychotherapy "bodies" or "the body" has meant literally, and simply, sex and the erotic. For others it's the preverbal: how mothers and babies communicate before talking takes over. For many it means somatisation—including illnesses, eating disorders, and unexplained physical symptoms. For others it means the myriad feelings, sensations and impulses that emerge in the countertransference. For some, the body is a cultural object fought over in a political war involving power, gender, sex, human rights, and aesthetics.

All these dimensions are relevant, yet none of these fully capture what body psychotherapists have meant by "the body". In this chapter I want to set out four modes of attending to the body that reflect the potential breadth and complexity of this process. This will include an overview of the contributions made by psychoanalysis, attachment theory, and neuroscience. I wish to elucidate both what contemporary body psychotherapy has to offer whilst also recognising the complex tensions of the history of ideas in psychotherapy. It is time to go beyond the tendency of both psychoanalytic and humanistic and integrative theorists to polarise and claim (implicitly or explicitly) concepts and practices as belonging solely to their own tradition.[1]

There has been a sea change in the field towards recognising the importance of the body in psychotherapy fuelled by interdisciplinary dialogue and advances in science (Carroll, 2003). Rather than summarise these, I want to share with you a series of metaphors from key writers that mark a progression beyond the dualistic idea of body and mind towards the idea of embodiment as a process within a relational context. The first is from the neurologist Damasio:

> The body, as represented in the brain, may constitute the indispensable frame of reference for the neural processes we experience as mind … our very organism [the body] is used as the *ground reference* for the constructions we make of the world around us and for the construction of the ever present sense of subjectivity. (1994, p. xviii)

The ground reference is the marking used on a landing strip to guide an airplane into land. Grounding is a term long associated with body psychotherapy: it means connecting to feelings and sensations in the body, and being in strong contact with the ground through the legs and feet. It emphasises the present moment. It often means slowing down a process.

The next metaphor catches the potential creativity and spontaneity of embodied relating. Neuroscientists Chiel and Beer writing about the feedback loop dynamics between the brain, body and environment compare them to the relationship between *"improvising musicians in a jazz ensemble"* (1997, p. 554; my italics). The point is that the brain is not the conductor of the orchestra, nor the executor controlling the actions of the body. Rather, brain and body, self and other, nervous system and environment, influence and respond to each other, "riffing" off each other as jazz musicians do.

We cannot directly observe changes in the brain but we can track a relational process by being aware of our own and our client's body. This is a complex and challenging task especially when, at the same time, we are listening to the client's words, managing our own responses, and formulating our thoughts. Totton describes how embodiment is "a process, not a state", which entails the "witnessing aspect of mind rhythmically leaping like a dolphin above the sea of the body" (2010). This third metaphor captures the way minds move between observation of, and immersion in, our experiential field.

Relationality and Mitchell's "modes"

Relationality involves the capacity both to think and hold multiple perspectives, and to perceive the other's body and to feel one's own body as a source of emotional aliveness and engagement. As the metaphors above suggest, this is a complex multifaceted process requiring both spontaneity and discipline, involving timings ranging between split-second perceptions and slower reflective responses (Carroll, 2005).

It is precisely the multiple aspects of this process that I want to differentiate in my discussion about working with the body in psychotherapy. I propose to use, as a framework for this, Stephen Mitchell's four "modes" of relating in his book *Relationality: From Attachment to Intersubjectivity* (2000).[2] In his description of four relational modes in psychotherapy I believe he captured something broader than new psychoanalytic trends. He differentiated aspects of therapeutic work that are applicable to all relational psychotherapies, and indeed all creative human relationships.

His four modes are akin to four lenses; four ways of perceiving the relational process. Mitchell defines them as:

- Non-reflective behaviour
- Affect permeability
- Self–other configuration
- Intersubjectivity

I have adapted this framework slightly to highlight the way in which attention to the body in psychotherapy can be understood, according to these modes, in quite distinct ways. Although Mitchell himself rarely refers directly to the body, this framework makes sense because the concept of embodiment and relationality go hand in hand. Furthermore, I hope to show how a grasp of these modes can be used to understand how we can deepen the therapeutic contact with the client.[3]

Mode One is non-reflective behaviour, which I am calling "procedural organisation". This refers to the observable aspects of human interaction: the way the client walks, sits, their manner of expression, gesture, posture, and the therapist's corresponding personal movement, vocabulary, habits, patterns. It also refers to timing and rhythm—coordination or lack of it with the other. It refers to the physical body and its organisation in space as fundamental to our sense of self and our implicit communication and exchange with others.

This is the area that body and movement psychotherapists such as Pat Ogden and Nick Totton have specialised in, developing a range of precise skills for working directly with embodied awareness and interaction. An interest in the procedural is now entering the mainstream as a result of infant–parent observation, the study of trauma, and a range of developments in neuroscience such as the discovery of mirror neurones.

Mode Two is affect permeability, which I am calling "affect (or emotion) regulation". This encompasses the whole range of human mood and affect that is felt, explored and elaborated in therapy. It includes the therapist's role in co- and self-regulation, conveying empathy, and identifying dissociation. Our capacity to do this depends on our willingness to be fully in touch with our own affective world. Second, it requires a good understanding of different developmental stages in the client's ability to own, digest and manage affects.

This is the common ground of most approaches to psychotherapy, and it is an area that has been given particular focus and developed theoretically in attachment theory (including the concept of mentalization), and approaches integrating neuroscience and relational thinking.

Mode Three is self–other configuration. This refers to symbolic aspects of self and other as they are evoked, enacted, and embodied in the therapeutic relationship. Historically, this has been understood as transference and countertransference. The crucial element is the use of the other as an object, however unconsciously or lightly this is held.

This is the heartland of psychoanalytic thinking: an understanding of bodies as sites of projection carrying symbolic meaning. It encompasses the construction, confusion or creations of self and other identity within the therapeutic relationship. The constructivists, both psychoanalytic and integrative, have extended this to include one's own body and others' bodies as cultural and political objects.

Mode Four is intersubjectivity. Mitchell (2000) defines this as "the mutual recognition of self-reflective, agentic persons" (p. 58). It involves the capacity to negotiate the paradoxical tension between the other as subject and object. In this context, the therapist's body and the client's body act as both resource and container for mutual meeting.

This is the realm of relational psychoanalysis, as well as contemporary integrative psychotherapy. It has roots in social and political theory, as well as infant research and developmental studies. It brings together the complexity of psychoanalytic thinking and the humanistic value of authenticity into a relational approach informed by a high level of reflexivity.

Mitchell's discussion of the modes was aimed both at setting theory in context and at examining therapeutic choices in practice. It is impossible to perceive in all four modes at once—they are simply different lenses—but we can move between them and make links between them. It is precisely in shifting between modes of participation that we can really work at clinical depth. Whatever we theorise or intuit about the client through our perception of their body and our own body, it is the therapeutic interaction that makes an impact. This is where I think Mitchell's "modes" have their greatest value—not in adding another theory, model or further abstraction but creating a framework to consider the focus of the actual clinical interventions.

I will use an extended clinical example that includes the use of touch with a client to show how these modes work in practice. Touch is a controversial intervention, and therefore I focus on illustrating where it fits into the broader embodied context of the therapy with this client. I do not think about the modes as I work, but in retrospect I find Mitchell's framework helps differentiate aspects of the therapeutic process as it unfolds moment to moment.

The modes in depth

Mode One: procedural organisation

I have replaced Mitchell's "non-reflective behaviour" with the term procedural organisation (a term he also uses in his description of this mode) to highlight the underlying intelligence, coherence and contingency of body responses in relational contexts (Bucci, 2008; Ogden, 2013).

The term "procedural" refers to the observable aspects of the physical body, and its operations in real time and space. Procedural memory includes everything we have learned on a bodily level—skills, habits, breathing patterns, expressiveness or inhibition, responses to trauma, and implicit relational "know how". It operates largely out of awareness unless we choose to focus on it. Procedural processes are implicit communications that run in parallel to verbal thinking and speech. They may confirm or complicate, or be quite dissociated from the words being spoken. A sudden change in pitch, a tilt of the head, a frown, the client's particular way of entering or leaving the room, are all procedurally organised.

Wilhelm Reich, the founder of body psychotherapy, anchored his theories in both procedural observation and his understanding of the nervous system (Eiden, 2009). "Procedural organisation" describes how the body's make-up—the motor system (muscles), the nervous systems,[4] the viscera, skin, and the senses—shapes, participates in, and is impacted by, the relational context (Fogel, 2009). A focus on procedural organisation has always been intrinsic to body psychotherapy; it is an essential part of what we have meant by "the body". Now, increasing understanding of the procedural nature of memory, of development and of human interaction is beginning to move "the body" from the periphery of psychology to the centre.

The "countertransference revolution" in psychoanalysis (Samuels, 1993), which started in the 1950s, evolved to give the therapist's body a privileged place in the profession as a source of critical information. Half a century later there are gradually expanding pockets in the psychoanalytic field with clinicians willing to upgrade the client's bodily experience from symptom/unconscious speech to an equally valued referential resource (Anderson, 2008).

"Procedural" shares roots with the term "process" and this is the key to understanding Mode One. Working procedurally in a psychotherapy context means tracking a process through observing it in the client's body and the body of the therapist, and linking it back into other aspects of what is being explored (Hartley, 2009). The felt, experienced or "lived" body becomes a vital and more explicit point of reference in the implicit dialogue.

Esther

My clinical illustration is based on work with a client I will call Esther; she has generously given permission for me to write about the therapy. When she first came to see me, Esther was going through a painful divorce. She needed to make sense of the turns her life had taken and she seemed determined to drive her development in therapy forward through the sheer force of inquiry and self-analysis. Esther was impatient for insight and knowledge: if she posed a question and I didn't answer instantly, she was off again, dispensing with me and formulating her own answers. She often spoke over me.

There were many dimensions to this difficulty with finding a jointly created rhythm, and as many ways to explore it. However, I want to focus on how a Mode One procedural approach could be linked with both Mode Two affect-regulation and the Mode Three symbolic configurations of self and other.

In the first year of our work we focused on making sense of her story and I supported her to pay attention to her body. Subsequently, I had begun to comment on the way she seemed compelled to fill the space with words, and was encouraging her just to notice what happened when she paused and allowed herself to breathe and make eye contact with me (Mode One procedural). Then one day, she began the session with a smile and said, "Hello—I have nothing particular to talk about, I have come empty …"

I responded by saying, "Yes, I notice that even your hello was different". I tried to capture the rising inflection of her "hello". She held eye contact with me, silent for some minutes and then said, "I feel like I am drinking you in" (a symbolic/Mode Three description of the procedural/Mode One process).

I nodded, and the silence continued as we savoured a mutual gaze. A palpable atmosphere of longing emerged. The sense of yearning was in her eyes, but her jaw—always tight—now seemed the focus of strain in the overall picture of her face. I was conscious of deliberately allowing myself to focus on her mouth as well as her eyes. After a while I said, "I was just noticing your jaw, and I feel like letting my own jaw soften a bit" (Mode One).

"I have tension there," she noted.

Her breathing deepened and there was an increasing sense of softness and letting go. Her face began to reveal a more sombre aspect.

Finally I said, "You are allowing me to see your sadness" (Mode Two affect).

Procedural process, though observable and pin-down-able, is very fast, complex, and intricate. The important thing to grasp about working therapeutically with the procedural mode is that it involves a very active phenomenological awareness. One aspect of this is a slowing down and focusing on the perception of specifics in the body in order to actually assimilate the sensation, structure and dynamic underlying habitual, sometimes highly charged, interactions.

Fritz Perls used the term "contact" to refer to the creative exchange or adjustment between one person and another (Clarkson & Mackewn, 1993). Contact is observable and variable, moment to moment, "a constant, richly informative play" (Houston, 2000, p. 20). In Chiron body psychotherapy we focused on the complexity of the procedural elements as an "energetic perception" reflecting the multilayeredness of the therapeutic relationship (Carroll, 2009). In another strand of development, Pat Ogden has expanded and updated the concept of contact, integrating it with attachment theory, neuroscience and trauma theory in sensorimotor psychotherapy (Ogden, Minton, & Pain, 2006).

Proprioception (literally "to receive oneself") is the technical name for the brain's registration of the body's movement in time and space; it is a crucial part of our felt sense. Helping the client be aware of gesture, breath, and especially sensation can focus experience and highlight the "edge", where critical affects, perceptions and memories can be caught in their precise dimensions (Preston, 2008). The process of tracking movement sequence and breathing can be unfamiliar, challenging, and demand a particular kind of concentration from the client, but its reward is an enhanced feeling for the client of being in one's body in the here and now (see Ogden's chapter in this volume). Explicit work with the body can support the development of self-agency in the client and enhance their ability to enter more fully into relationship.

> In the next session we expanded this exploration of faces and gazing, as I encouraged Esther to become aware of the position of her chin. She began to notice the sensation and the feelings that accompanied her characteristic way of keeping her chin high (Mode One). Soon she started playing with the different symbolic meanings of "chin up"; the most resonant was the phrase "keeping my head above water" (Mode Three). I invited her just to stay in eye contact, feeling how her chin wanted to go up. She experimented with lowering it an inch or so whilst holding my gaze. After a while she started crying. "This is so intimate", she said.

Tracking micro-movements gives direct feedback on how the relational dynamic is unfolding. One day I was encouraging Esther with a comment about how she was breaking new ground with her adult daughters; they had been very rejecting of her since the divorce and she was struggling to improve her relationship with them. She did not pause to take in my comment and I observed her chin pull back and lift slightly. I proceeded to explore the impact of my comment. She was able to notice an underlying fear, "can I trust it?" (Mode Two). She became aware that her raised chin was linked with the image of being on guard in her "ivory tower". In the following session we stayed with the theme of exploring how she held her head, and she noticed the shyness she experienced "when words are not there to protect me" (Modes One and Two). She became absorbed in scanning my face, remembering how she used to try to read her mother's face (Mode Three). The following week she revealed, "When I went home, I had an image of your face—I lay down and cried. It is something I have never experienced before".

A further critical factor in understanding the role of the body in psychotherapy has come from the use of film. Since the 1970s the use of video has played a critical role in enabling researchers to break down and study the subtle dynamic interplay between mothers and babies (Stern, 1985; Trevarthen & Aitken, 2001). Facial expression, micro-movements, rhythmic patterns, vocal changes, shifts of gaze and various combinations of phenomena have been analysed.

Beebe, who gave the John Bowlby Memorial Lecture for the Bowlby Conference in 2001, has been a pioneer in bringing the fruits of her infant research directly into technical aspects of her relational work with adult clients. She comments that "Relating ... requires that one have more or less continuous feedback about the state of the other" (Beebe & Lachmann, 2002, p. 99). Beebe's explorations of the phenomenology of self and other regulation is part of a movement that also includes the work of the Boston Change Study Group and that is now influencing contemporary psychotherapy. (Beebe, Knoblauch, Rustin, & Sorter, 2003)

The choreography of each therapeutic relationship is unique, and can, in and of itself, underpin at different times impasse, enactment, aliveness, steady change, or dramatic transformation (La Barre, 2001).

We may catch a client's gesture, posture, facial expression, or tone of voice and heighten the client's awareness of it by playing it back to them or encouraging them to play with it, to amplify it, or elaborate it. Body psychotherapist Yorai Sella explains that "The establishment and maintenance of a sense of meaning is dependent upon a bodily and energetic experience which has gained an internal cohesiveness", enabling a "good enough sensory congruence [between] internal or external events" (Sella, 2005, p. 89).

Procedural work focuses on the quality of an interaction and the immediacy of participation. Sometimes it is about inviting spontaneity, or getting through to a client whose implicit way of being feels very hard to penetrate. Recently there has been an increasing interest in improvisation as an aspect of relational psychoanalysis (Ringstrom, 2001). Body, movement, drama and creative arts therapies have specialised in facilitating the client to expand their expressive range through the use of movement, sound, and gesture. The exploration and negotiation of space is intrinsic to this kind of relational work. Movement exploration, bodywork, setting up and playing out a particular scene and using materials and objects may all be incorporated to discover new dimensions to experience.

Rhythm is central to procedural organisation and client and therapist co-create certain rhythms of being together, reflecting many aspects of their relationship (Carroll, 2005). The therapist may synchronise with the client's movements, or counterpoint with a different rhythm, or deliberately pause for reflection to hold the tension. The therapist's attunement to the client may be reflected in the way they match or modify the client's rhythm: slowing down to soothe, or speeding up to enliven and to stimulate, or using humour to invite playfulness. This kind of contingent mirroring (Fonagy, Gergely, Jurist & Target, 2002) is at the heart of developing new relational and emotional capacities.

Mode Two: affect regulation

In *Descartes' Error* Damasio wrote "Feeling is not an elusive mental quality attached to an object, but rather the direct perception of a specific landscape—that of the body" (1994, p. xvi). Neuroscience has now established that areas of the brain concerned with affect overlap with the structures that represent and regulate body states (Damasio, 1994; Panksepp, 1998). We are bound to resonate with others' feelings because our inbuilt capacities for emotion detection and evaluation actually use the same parts of the brain for perceiving others' feelings as it does to register our own (Gallese, 2009). Whatever the therapeutic background or training we bring to our clinical practice, when we are working with the range of human emotions and how they manifest in the therapeutic relationship, we are implicitly if not explicitly working with the body.

Mitchell defines Mode Two "affect permeability" as "shared experience of intense affect across permeable boundaries." I am broadening this perspective and using the term affect regulation for Mode Two. This implies not just that affects in one person impact and influence another, but also that the art of regulating affect is a central process of psychotherapy (Schore, 2003).

As human beings we are all born with the capacity to experience love, hate, rage, joy, fear, excitement, disgust, desire, envy, playfulness, and more. The clues to our client's affective states come from context, content, procedural cues, and from the client's narrative style. However, Mode Two is also often registered strongly through perceptions of our own internal state. This is not surprising, since a great deal of information about our emotions comes via interoception, the perception of our visceral state and the neurochemical changes in the body (Craig, 2002). As therapists we are trained to recognise mood and affect, and that sensitivity often shows up first as a response in our own body, which acts as a kind of resonating chamber. Various clinical terms are used to describe how our clients' feelings impact and trigger our own—resonance, projective identification, countertransference, mutual dissociation. I identify these processes as central to Mode Two, distinguishing them from the specific observation of externals, which characterises Mode One, even though there is obviously an overlap between them.

In contemporary integrative and psychoanalytic therapies it is recognised that clients need to feel their feelings in order for change to occur; and that we need to work carefully and thoughtfully to support this (Orbach, 2005). This is particularly important as we recognise that dissociation may well be in operation in the client and in the therapist. Part of our role may be to hold the fragments—picking up hidden or dissociated affect in imagery, free association, bodily clues in the client, or sensations within our own body. This feeds into how we help the client find the words for feelings, make sense of them and, crucially, validate feelings. In a relational approach there is an increasing emphasis on therapist's use of their own affective response to help the client become aware of the impact they make (Maroda, 2010).

In her study of the regulation of affect between parents and infants, and psychotherapists and their clients, Beebe named three dimensions of affect regulation: heightened affective moments, ongoing regulations, rupture and repair (Beebe & Lachman, 2002). This view encompasses a range of possibilities for direct emotional engagement between client and therapist. It highlights the fundamental process of interactive regulation as part of "ongoing regulations", which goes hand in hand with the role of repairing failures of attunement that result in rupture. The heightened affective moment—whether it occurs as part of an enactment, or the culmination of support for the client to allow their feelings full expression—can become a critical moment of growth and change (Carroll, 2003). Porges' polyvagal theory enhances our understanding of how optimal relational engagement directly affects the nervous system (Porges, 2011).

This requires the procedural skills referred to in the previous section and also the therapist's capacity to bear a wide range of affects, which may be complex. Affects can creep in quietly, or burst into awareness, and electrify or deaden contact. They may be experienced as disruptive or painful though they can also be vigorously life-affirming. In a relational exploration, emotions that may never have been held in awareness and attended to may become more textured, meaningful and bearable for the client, and for the therapist. In this way, as Mitchell remarks, "Affects, on higher levels of organisation, [may become] folded into a subjective sense of agency" (2000, p. 70).

> In the first phase of my work with Esther I had an image of her powering along like a speedboat, leaving a wake of choppy foamy waves of rage, guilt, fear, panic, grief and loneliness eddying round the room. I felt her urgency, and a sense of shock, in my own body as I struggled to remain anchored and stay with her. Her ceaseless narrative driving through the session seemed impervious to my input. At some point I named the terrible loneliness she had buried under a lifelong facade of activity and coping (Mode Two). She often referred back to that session, and what she calls the "two bombs"—the words "loneliness" and "panic".
>
> One day she asked if I thought she needed antidepressants. Her sleep had been disturbed and she was anxious. I said I thought she was afraid that I might not stay with her through these strong feelings. I commented, "In your eyes I can see the fear that no one

will come, but I am here" (Mode Two and Three). I wondered aloud if she had always been living with panic, and it was now more conscious. This prompted a burst of urgent questions: who are you to me? Are we mother and baby? (Mode Three) How can my needs be met here? Exploration of this kept her loneliness in the foreground. She became angry with me as she felt her helplessness and intense grief. She brought me a symbolic six boxes of tissues for all the tears she felt needed crying, for sixty years of loneliness and for her many losses, especially the lack of connection to her mother.

As Esther began to grieve actively there were changes in her breathing and posture. What was also noticeable was how she became more able to pause occasionally, to look at me, to reconnect. But the element of crisis was highlighted in her dreams of being displaced, dispossessed, and abandoned. She dreamt of seeing her sister with their parents on the beach whilst she remained in the shadows hiding. In another dream she is attacked by a friend, who runs off, leaving her without handbag or keys (Mode Three). Bromberg writes about dreams of robbery as a metaphor for loss of control; these frequently occur "at a transitional point, where the patient is beginning to surrender his dissociative structure and is shifting to a more conflicted one" (2001, p. 217).

Esther's conflict centred on the (relative) safety of disconnecting from her loneliness compared with the risk of reaching out for connection and exposing her vulnerability. It was at this point that I started focusing on her eye contact with me, and how she held her head (described in the previous section). However, unless held in strong interactive regulation—such as when I explicitly directed her towards slowing down and connecting with me—she tended to dissociate (Mode One and Two). For example, she might allude to her desire for more connection to others but immediately dismiss it or switch to another subject. I decided that one way to make that desire something we could explore directly was to be open to moments in which we could explore her tentative reaching for support or comfort with me. (In her chapter in this volume, Ogden discusses such gestures as "proximity-seeking actions.")

Such a moment came in one session as I was asking her how she experienced what she described as "yearning", and specifically how she felt it in her body (Mode One and Two). She started to stroke herself, and speak about how she wanted to be stroked.

This was the first time she had made the link between her feelings, her body, and her relational needs. Gradually, we approached her tentative longing for "someone" to stroke her arms (Mode Three). I wondered how it might feel for that "someone" to be me. I proceeded very slowly asking her to notice how she felt as I moved my chair closer. I was observing her breathing closely for signs that the pace of this process might be overwhelming (i.e., chest breathing or holding her breath) (Mode One). Once I was sitting within touching distance she had a sense that she simply wanted me to make contact on her upper arm and hold it. When my hand rested on her arm and my eyes made contact with hers, she described it as "like being held—a bandage on my heart" (Mode Three).

Despite its name—mentalization—the concept of the capacity to make sense of one's own mind and others' minds depends crucially on the skill of self and other body awareness, as well as the ability to imagine another's point of view. Alienation from the body is a product of early relational breakdown that renders experience as intensity of affect without meaning or without relief and resolution (Sella, 2005). Bowlby's study of attachment, and the subsequent developments in attachment theory, demonstrates why and how affects are unconsciously dissociated or amplified to serve the need to maintain a connection to a parent (Cassidy & Shaver, 1999).

The necessary corollary to the process of resonating with and acknowledging feelings is the skill of being able to collaborate with the client in making sense of them. "Mentalization is centrally concerned with appreciating emotional truth, allowing different perspectives but anchoring them in the evidence of actual feeling and direct experience, as well as in the capacity to imagine what could be different" (Target, 2008, p. 278). Part of my aim in focusing on Esther's yearning for connection was to soften the rather brittle, judgemental quality that tended to permeate her evaluation of her own and others' emotion. As long as her vulnerability was dissociated and avoided, so too was her ability to make an empathic connection with herself and others.

Mentalising is a cumulative process, requiring right-brain implicit communication as well as engagement in an explicit attempt at meaning-making and perspective-taking. The process of identifying meanings is tricky and non-linear; as Mitchell observes, "Our emotions and our behaviours have, to some degree, a messy life of their own, in the gaps, the spaces, between oneself and the others" (2000, p. 69). We get affectively entangled even as we try to scaffold emerging links and build increasing coherence in the co-created narrative.

Nevertheless "affect regulation" is an embodied skill that can be learned and developed in therapy. For some therapists this might sound too close to a medical model. Yet there is room for a wider interpretation. Affect regulation is about finding optimal aliveness, broadening the range of feelings experienced, as well as tempering pain and distress.

Mode Three: self–other configuration

In psychoanalysis the idea of the psychotherapy setting as a container of multiple levels of reality has a long history. With the developments in relational psychoanalysis this concept becomes more fluid and bidirectional, and the emphasis shifts to multiple self-states (Bromberg, 2001). The democratising of the therapeutic space (paralleled in the Gestalt concept of field theory) is perhaps the reason why Mitchell chose to call Mode Three "self–other configurations" rather than "transference–countertransference".

With self–other configuration we move into the realm of the symbolic, imaginative, limitless possibilities of meaning and interpretation; towards enactment and potential space. Laplanche states that "the human subject is a theorizing being ... a self-symbolizing-being" (1989, p. 10). In this mode the body is anything and everything; it is constructed and co-constructed. Our own body and others' bodies may be used and abused, manipulated in fantasy and reconfigured creatively to define and redefine our identity (Butler, 1993). This perspective has been developed most notably by Susie Orbach, who gave the John Bowlby Memorial Lecture for the Bowlby Conference in 2003. Objectification of one's own body and others' bodies may range from a cultural norm through eating disorders to extremes of body dysmorphia, or violence towards others (Orbach, 2010).

Working with self–other configurations requires the therapist to hold in reserve their immediate responses in order to discover in what ways they are being constructed as an object by the client. As Orbach puts it,

> I am curious about what my body may have to offer to the bodies of my patients ... In what ways can my body be of value to my patient? How can they use it as a site of provision, as a site of identification, as a site of stability or as a site of projection? (2006, p. 70)

This reserve entails a surrender to, a tolerance of, or just survival of the other's projections. A client may arrive certain that he will be humiliated for who he is and what he brings. That fear of impending humiliation will fuel a vigilant search for danger: anything in the therapist's demeanour, timing or phrasing may trigger the sense of history repeating itself. At other times the therapist may be sought as an ideal object, bringing balm to the client's anxious state. Or the co-creation of self and other configurations may be more playful, erotic, or confrontational.

Self–other configurations draw on a vast reservoir that both therapist and client bring to their encounter; a reservoir of personal history and cultural images. This memory bank of self-and-other images is not exactly "stored" in the brain or the body, but rather may be evoked implicitly or recalled through association. The neuroscientist Llinas compares this process to "sympathetic chords", internal resonances that are self-activating (Llinas & Churchland, 1997). As Peters observes, "there is an almost infinite subtlety in living processes and how information is encoded and flows through us" (2000, p. 46).

Bucci argues that imagery is the pivot of the process that connects subsymbolic (i.e., procedural and affective) with verbal and symbolic referential processes (2008). Imagery—whether it is a metaphor, a formal symbol, or an imagined scenario of self and other—has the capacity to pick up information from the body on the penumbra of awareness. This may elaborate into a creative expression capturing the total gestalt of the relational moment. Noticing a client's spontaneous images or scenarios, or asking for their image of a situation, symptom, or feeling, can of itself be a way to implicitly invite a symbolic elaboration of sensory material. How we make sense of this as it unfolds through a process of encounter and enactment is another critical dimension of the psychotherapeutic process.

> Some months later we were exploring Esther's new mood of self-acceptance. She was more settled in her life and I said something like, "There's nothing to deal with except being here with me". She blushed and looked slightly sideways out of her eyes at me,

commenting shyly on the pleasure of being here. It was hard for her to stay with that moment, and she started to speak rapidly about a younger woman she had been friends with. I sought to link her embarrassment and excitement back to us (Mode Two and Three). As she was leaving the session she suddenly embraced me and kissed me fervently on the cheek.

When she came back the next time, feeling shame and humiliation at her "crossing boundaries", I acknowledged her anxiety and sought to explore what lay behind her impulse (Mode Two and Three). Could there be hope and excitement behind it as well as some rebellion against the limits of therapy? I wanted to convey curiosity and openness rather than alarm, as the embrace felt to me more like a moment of confusion about how to share her joy. It proved a fruitful enactment because the feelings it unearthed were complex. She felt angry that I had not protected her from strong feelings, including sexual feelings. I asked what was evoked last week by my exploration of her pleasure in being with me (Mode Three). I also wondered whether my touching her arm a few months previously had felt sexual. She said it had not, though related this to a more general feeling of being frustrated and of wanting to be able to "dance" to "flow with her body". Her confusion was around how safe it was to be spontaneous, and the fear of a mismatch between us about what was appropriate. I acknowledged the heightened charge and suggested there was something precious in these moments of aliveness and I hoped they would not go underground.

In the following session she came back saying she felt vulnerable, but wanted to explore "the movement back and forth" between us. With her anxiety rising, she rapidly moved off the topic, and I sat forward, encouraging her to stay with what she had brought. I commented on her chin rising up (Mode One), and she immediately thought back to "keeping her head above water". Then she said, "I don't want to approach through a window or chimney—I want to come in through the front door" (Mode Three symbolic). She leaned forward to hold my hand, which I gave and she said "you are real". She held my hands and my gaze for a few minutes, and I had a sense of her trying to assemble a new thought. Finally she said, "This is not sex. Sex happens in the dark. It is being an object, touching but not looking."

We were negotiating multiple shifting self–other configurations in this moment: both re-evoking and undoing patterns of intrusion, of covert sexual encounters, of emotional starvation, of secrecy and objectification (Mode Three). The simultaneity of old and emergent ways of being with another, combined with the client's fierce desire to know and understand, enabled her to chisel out a fresh perspective. There was a lot to talk about in relation to her sexual experiences, the messages about sex from her family and in her culture. We also discussed the differences between psychoanalytic and body psychotherapy (she was reading Kristeva and Winnicott). Questions arose in her, and also in me, which I took to supervision. Is this therapy, or is this playing? Is she stealing or am I seducing? (Mode Three) Was her separation anxiety exacerbated by my decision to occasionally include touch?

I felt elements of both pre-oedipal and oedipal desires were being constellated, and I was conscious we were exploring a delicate, potentially explosive area of self–other relating (Asheri, 2009). In a subsequent session we explored holding hands again, sitting opposite each other (Mode One). She was holding on strongly. I felt it in my belly: an intense, fixed hold on me. I shared my sense that she did not want to let go of me. Her talking had become disconnected from her strong grip and I asked her to notice what she was feeling (Mode Two). "It's hard to go", she said, holding tight as she began to cry. In the next session she was able to laugh at herself "I am very stubborn. I didn't have a self before. Now I do and I can say—I am very gentle, and very aggressive".

Throughout these weeks of intense exploration of the arousal level in the room, I was aware of the danger of seeming to tease her with the potential for touch, yet I felt it was important for me to trust my sense that what was emerging was a genuine striving for connection and contact. Her excitement seemed to belong to the process of entering new territory of intimacy—of looking, of asking, of being seen and responded to, of boldness and experiment and of changing expectations (Mode Three).

We can understand enactment as a process which operates potentially in all modes. There is a dialectical tension between procedural process and self–other configuration. We cannot track in both modes simultaneously, though we can shift our attention between them. In Mode

Three the bodies of self and other are perceived indirectly—they are dreamt up, elaborated, and used to elucidate what may be unspoken or as yet unformulated. A procedural detail may set off a cascade of memories and feelings, and therapist and client may surrender voluntarily or involuntarily to the tidal sweep of re-enactment (Soth, 2005).

For Bromberg, enactment represents the client's unconscious longing to be known in this place of "not-me" (2011). It's because of the risks of this—the risk of losing a therapeutic position or failing to contain the clients process—that for so long psychoanalysis prescribed a more detached stance. It is one reason why touch has been a strict taboo in psychotherapy. As a body psychotherapist, I maintain the possibility of working with touch with some clients at certain times. One prerequisite for me in deciding to use touch is that the client and I have established a relationship where we have developed a practice of exploring procedural interaction. I cannot know in advance what touch will mean for *this* client, in *this* moment, but I can monitor my own responses closely and keep a dialogue going with the client about the touch itself (Asheri, 2009).

Bromberg argues that:

> Dissociated domains of self achieve symbolization primarily through enactment ... because experience becomes symbolized not by words [and interactions] themselves but by the new perceptual context that the words [and interactions] come to represent". (Bromberg 2001, p. 256)[5]

As Esther herself said: "You are real". In other words, the actual grasp—the actual skin to skin contact—became meaningful in a new way, as a connection with an other grounded in the here and now.

> Within a few months the sessions started to feel lighter, more playful, and varied in tone and texture. One day Esther came in with lots to talk about—her new piano, an argument with her brother, a conversation about suffering. It was quite lively and at one point as she went back to her old habit of talking over me. I had to say, "Listen—I am trying to say something ..." She sat back, putting her feet up on the footstool. We spoke about the difficulty of play, and I noticed her feet moving excitedly as she talked. I said, "Your

feet are moving ... they are good at play". "They are far from my head", she joked.

She started the following session by telling me she had dreamt of her daughter Rebecca as a toddler. She is with a childminder and Esther is just observing, until Rebecca says "mum" and sticks her foot out for her to put her sock on (Mode Three). She went into a deeper analysis of the dream and I noticed that her feet were moving. She segued into a more philosophical mode about suffering and loss, but I was more preoccupied with her feet, and I said after a while, "There are two things going on at once—you are 'doing therapy' and your feet are moving. I wonder if you really feel more like playing than talking?" (Mode Two). She gave me a look that was mischievous and slightly self-conscious.

For a few seconds I thought hard about how to stay with this aliveness. Suddenly, I thought of an exercise I do with groups which is fun and yet challenging. It involves people in pairs standing opposite each other holding either end of a chopstick with the pads of their fingers (Mode One). It encourages non-verbal attunement because both people have to sense the right amount of pressure to use and constantly adjust as they move around the room. They need to coordinate their movements as they improvise with different shapes. The moment optimum contact pressure on the chopsticks is lost, they fall to the ground.

I wondered how Esther would manage, given her difficulties with coordinating timing and intensity. In fact she loved it and amazed me by moving strongly and quickly forward (chasing me into the corner) and back, so I had to move fast to stop the chopsticks falling. "Who is leading and who is following?" she asked. My sense was that she was leading the dance and I had to rally a matching intensity to keep up! She was keen to experiment too—adding more chopsticks, closing her eyes. We tried holding the chopsticks with our toes (and failed). We laughed and laughed. We sat back down in our chairs near the end of the session. She analysed the process and concluded, "It's like a dialogue". "Indeed", I said.

At the next session, there were three significant markers of change. Esther brought in a book of Escher's illustrations. She said, "My perception has shifted—I see the white birds now rather than the black" (Mode Three). She was referring to feeling more optimistic, but I was also struck by the fact that the point of Escher's pictures are that there is more than one perspective, and they often have a strong two-way current, a back and forth.

Then she told me she had dreamt of her other daughter, Judit as a toddler jumping onto her lap and standing there. They meet in a moment of joyous strong eye contact. She told me that when Judit was a baby she had not been able to enjoy gazing at her and that the dream felt like a gift. I was struck by the way the dream image highlighted eyes and feet. The toddler is supported, and fully engaged with her mother—a robust energy regulated in a strong attuned contact. The dream condensed ideas of relational and developmental healing between mother and daughter (Mode Three), echoing the energy and modality of the meeting of feet, of eyes and of hands in our recent work.

As we continued to explore the dream I commented on its link to her mother, "You couldn't see that she loved you, it wasn't in her body language—so you had to earn it." Recalling a model scene of herself at the swimming pool, trying to dive dramatically to get her mother's attention, Esther said, "My mum's body is saying leave me alone, I am tired, your energy reminds me of your dad, I have other kids, I am exhausted and I have nothing to give". This was the first time in the therapy Esther had ever projected herself into another's mind and given them a first-person voice, rather than her third—person dry and often critical account of another's behaviour. She had made a leap spontaneously into the perspective of another, without losing a sense of her own feelings of loss.

Mode Four: intersubjectivity

Mitchell defines Mode Four, intersubjectivity, as "the mutual recognition of self-reflective, agentic persons" (2001, p. 58). In this, he is specifically drawing on the work of Jessica Benjamin who has focused on the paradoxical tension of negotiating subject-object relating and subject-subject relating. The distinction between this and the other modes is that the therapist is not just holding a process but is an overtly involved participant; he or she is called out or comes out into a more visible space as a subject. Mitchell writes about intersubjective engagement as a fulcrum for change, and one key aspect of this being the therapist's responsible use of expressiveness or restraint in their interactions (2001, p. 127).

I want to emphasise that this use of the term intersubjectivity is distinct from other uses of the word—for example, to refer to the inborn propensity of humans to seek relationship; or, the wide use of it to refer to the unconscious interplay between therapist and client. This latter view of intersubjectivity belongs more to Mode Three self–other configurations.

Feminism, philosophy (especially Buber), Gestalt psychotherapy and postmodernism have contributed to the theory of intersubjectivity as dialogical relating. It is not simply a theoretical but rather a political perspective that emphasises diversity of experience and the importance of recognising the subjectivity of the other. It acknowledges the dialectical tensions of moving between what Buber succinctly described as I-It and I-Thou relating (1958).

From my perspective Mitchell's "intersubjective" mode builds on and extends some basic humanistic and integrative principles, such as presence, authenticity, congruence, and the idea of "healing through meeting" (Buber, 1958). Here we start from the rich potential of embodied presence, of connection with an other who is truly "there" and is willing to be honestly involved and available for dialogue in the here and now (Jacobs, 2009).

An implicit moment of intersubjectivity is marked by a shift in the quality of embodiment—a threshold has been crossed and there is a palpable charge, an aliveness in both client and therapist. Often this seems to parallel the speaking of a truth that has been previously hidden or dissociated. There is a sense of immediacy, and a shift to a more intimate and less role-bound connection.

> In subsequent weeks, Esther and I continued to elaborate the theme of seeing and being seen along many parameters—with her daughters, with me, with the idea of finding a new partner. This was still a phenomenological relational process, as I continued to track the shifting pattern of dissociation and contact. In one session she was talking about her longing for a relationship—"I cannot reach it but I can see it," she said, referring to watching other couples. She drifted into a state of reverie, trying to imagine herself with a new partner. We began to trace and flesh out her hopes and desires. Sometime later as I asked her more about the detail of what she

was experiencing (Mode One and Two), she said, "It is something to do with your body, with being aware of your whole body and my longing for physical closeness". We talked about how the idea of being snuggled against a body is linked with feeling loved. She started to compare me with a port, and herself as Odysseus coming home (Mode Three). I felt deeply moved and I really had a sense of a sea change between us, a deep affective contact. Through a more powerful inner connection to herself, she stirred a stronger feeling in my heart as well (Mode Two).

Finally, I want to describe a session where we are still talking about touch and boundaries, and misreadings, and I am trying to hold the complexity of exploring closeness and sexuality when touch is a possibility in our work, and yet only one element of it. I comment on a recent episode she described with her daughter, when she restrained herself from taking her daughter's hand, and waited instead for her daughter to initiate the contact. She told me about learning to text and how this was a new dimension to that relationship. As she was talking about Judit, Esther was moving her whole body, smiling, and talking. I said, "It's good to see you like this—you look so—alive". And then found myself adding, "As I say this, I feel tearful". She had tears in her eyes too and said, "I know why you said that, why that makes you cry, because you are pleased to see me looking happy".

"Yes I am", I replied.

As the session continued, I was still considering in my own mind how to respond to the playful, the passionate and the vulnerable and hungry parts of her, whilst observing closely how I was affected by her body and her movements, moment to moment. She was articulating her own struggle between arriving at the depressive position (her choice of term), accepting the limits of therapy and life, not having a partner, and another more lively subversive impulse to know how far she could go. I said, "What I am noticing is that when your vulnerability is apparent, the idea of touch seems potentially nurturing or supportive. But I also notice that when you are excited, which I see in the way your body is moving around, I feel there is something more sexual here—and it makes me wonder what touch would mean then" (Modes Two and Three). A bit later, I added, "Today I am aware of these two parts of you—vulnerable and excitable", and Esther shot back, "Vulnerable and naughty!"

I was aware of the many months that we had negotiated, considered, skirted around or talked frankly about touch. I recalled a story about the ending of a close friendship with her friend Myra. Myra had said, rather damningly, using her hands as markers, "You want this high, but sometimes you just have to accept this high". Esther had experienced this as a rejection of her passion and eagerness. I said I was recalling the story of Myra and thinking about me and her now, "You want to aim this high", I said, illustrating with my hand the higher level.

"Yes", she laughed.

My story of Esther stops before the end of our work, but we are on a journey in which the possibility of my existing as a subject with and for her becomes more palpable. This occurs implicitly as she allows me more space in the dialogue and I notice more complex nuanced qualities in our eye contact; and explicitly as I share more of my dilemmas and responses with her openly and directly. In allowing her to see my feeling tearful I was surrendering to my own vulnerability in her presence for the first time. I was touched by the strong charge of mother–daughter love being rekindled in them after a long hiatus, and its resonance with my own experiences. Esther's immediate recognition of my feelings, and mine of hers, was a significant moment hovering on a cusp between Mode Two, shared affect, and Mode Four, intersubjectivity (mutual recognition). I say "on the cusp" because she is perhaps experiencing a confirmation of her own feelings rather than necessarily perceiving me as a subject.

The modes are neither hierarchical nor do they not unfold in a linear way. Nevertheless, the capacity of therapist and client to experience moments of mutual recognition often occur as a result of developmental change within the relationship over time. With Esther I went through many phases in the negotiation of a shared space that involved work in all four modes. Mutual recognition depends on the capacity of therapist and client to both resonate with, and differentiate from, the experience of the other. In this way the body can function as a mediator—a "third"— which can be used in the reflexive process (Aron, 2006).

The clinician who is secure in their relationship with their own body can develop the capacity to differentiate their habitual positions from the spontaneous emergence of a relational shift. Asheri emphasises that in order to do this, therapists need to be as familiar as they consciously can be with their own habitual relational positions and the developmental wounds that created them (2009). They may then recognise the contextual cue for a more active use of relational agency in the form of visceral information, which feeds into their reflexive processing. This then informs the intervention. Timing is critical because it involves a consideration of the client's need for a subject as opposed to the need for an object in that moment. As Asheri puts it, "the extent to which we embody our understanding of the relational dynamic experientially and the interest we have in the mutual impact that is occurring between the client and therapist is critical to holding the creative tension of the intersubjective engagement" (Asheri, 2007).

There is much more to Mode Four than I can convey here, and my clinical illustration illustrates just one facet of the potential of intersubjectivity. What I take from Mitchell and Asheri is that Mode Four involves an intentional stance towards the client of being willing to be available and open as a subject, whilst also being scrupulous in monitoring the timing and value of doing so. Sometimes this happens when the therapist feels actually quite cornered in a dynamic and has to find a way to break through to another mode of participation. These can be dramatic moments of confrontation or reconfiguration of perception, as Mitchell's own examples illustrate. This requires crucial therapeutic judgement relating to the therapist's explicit use of their own subjectivity to address impasses, dilemmas, and moments of heightened emotional connection. It may mean stepping into power, or surrendering to powerlessness; it may mean being willing to own and bear shame with the client, rather than defensively focusing on the client's issues. At times both parties must be prepared to risk going to their edge. "We can both potentially be changed by this engagement, if we can keep negotiating the multiplicity of our reality, moment to moment" (Asheri, 2009, p. 111).

Conclusion

In this extended clinical example I have tried to show how "working with the body" in a relational way involves holding the tension between very specific procedural elements and the wider context of attachment history with its repetitions and elaborations in the therapeutic relationship. It is impossible to include all the dimensions of the therapeutic work in one narrative, especially the continual reflexive processing that it entails. My intention has been to convey how a contemporary relational approach to the body is multifaceted, encompassing symbolic, affective and intersubjective aspects. Some elements of the way I work with the body reflect my body psychotherapy training; other aspects are common to many approaches in psychotherapy; and the influence of relational psychoanalysis is also important.

I would like to return now to the metaphors I laid out at the beginning. The body can be used as a ground reference, particularly through procedural work but also through acknowledging in a matter of fact way "this is what I feel" and through meeting the other in a grounded dialogue. The rich elaborative aspects of self-and-therapist configurations are played out in their imagined bodies in a continuous improvisation of familiar and novel scenes. Finally, reflexivity, which is an essential element of a relational psychotherapy, and a relational approach to the body, can be understood as the capacity to shift fluidly and frequently between immersion in, and observation of, the experiential field. Bodies in relation operate on a dynamic continuum of dissociation and embodied presence. As the scope of the clinical use of mutual dissociation is developed; as enactment is understood in its procedural dimension; and as working directly with the body becomes more common, I hope we are witnessing—and this book testifies to—a further seachange in the psychotherapy field towards embodied relational psychotherapies.[6]

Notes

1. Whilst the polemics, discussions and differentiations go on in and between schools at the conceptual level, the working practices of psychotherapists from a variety of backgrounds often have much more overlap than is publicly recognised.
2. Mitchell gave a paper on Attachment and Relationality for the John Bowlby Memorial Conference in 1998, which was later revised and included in his book, which I have taken as a seminal influence.
3. I am enormously indebted to my colleague Shoshi Asheri with whom I developed some of these ideas as part of our joint teaching work. Her personal warmth and support, critical thinking and rigorous ethic and practice has been an ongoing inspiration.
4. This refers to the neuroendocrine, autonomic and central nervous systems, which are intertwined and yet have specific roles in the regulation of affect and sensory perception.

5. I have changed Bromberg's own emphasis here and italicised "the new perceptual context" and added "interaction" in square brackets.
6. I also wish to thank Anne Marie Keary, Susan Law and Suzette Clough for their feedback and encouragement. And not least, Jon Blend, for his vigorous engagement with the writing of this chapter at various stages.

References

Anderson, F. S. (2008). *Bodies in Treatment: the Unspoken Dimension*. Hillsdale, NJ: Analytic Press.
Aron, L. (1996). *A Meeting of Minds: Mutuality in Psychoanalysis*. Hillsdale, NJ: Analytic Press.
Aron, L. (2006). Analytic impasse and the third: clinical implications of inter-subjectivity theory. *International Journal of Psychoanalysis, 87*: 349–368.
Asheri, S. (2007). Negotiating a sense of aliveness in the therapeutic relationship: an embodied intersubjective experience. A paper presented at the Chiron Association for Body Psychotherapists' conference on "Relational Dilemmas and Opportunities" in September 2007.
Asheri, S. (2009). To touch or not to touch: a relational body perspective. In: L. Hartley (Ed.), *Contemporary Body Psychotherapy: The Chiron Approach* (pp. 106–120). Abingdon: Routledge.
Asheri, S. (2013). Stepping into the void of dissociation: a therapist and client in search of a meeting place. In: J. Yellin, & O. Badouk Epstein (Eds.), *Terror Within and Without, Attachment and Disintegration: Working on the Edge* (pp. 73–89). London: Karnac.
Beebe, B., & Lachman, F. (2002). *Infant Research and Adult Treatment: Co-constructing Interactions*. Hillsdale, NJ: Analytic Press.
Beebe, B. Knoblauch, S. Rustin, J., & Sorter, D. (2003). *Forms of Intersubjectivity in Infant Research and Adult Treatment*. New York: Other Press.
Bromberg, P. (2001). *Standing In the Spaces: Essays on Clinical Process, Trauma and Dissociation*. Hillsdale, NJ: Analytic Press.
Bromberg, P. M. (2011). *The Shadow of the Tsunami and the Growth of the Relational Mind*. Abingdon: Routledge.
Buber, M. (1958 [1937]). *I and Thou* (Trans. R. G. Smith). New York: Scribner's.
Bucci, W. (2008). The role of bodily experience in emotional organisation. In: F. S. Anderson, *Bodies in Treatment: The Unspoken Dimension* (pp. 51–76). Hillsdale, NJ: Analytic Press.
Butler, J. P. (1993). *Bodies that Matter: On the Discursive Limits of Sex*. Abingdon: Routledge.

Carroll, R. (2003). On the border between chaos and order: neuroscience and psychotherapy. In: J. Corrigal, & H. Wilkinson (Eds.), *Revolutionary Connections: Neuroscience and Psychotherapy* (pp. 191–211). London: Karnac.

Carroll, R. (2005). Rhythm, re-orientation and reversal: deep re-organisation of the self in psychotherapy. In: J. Ryan, (Ed.), *How Does Psychotherapy Work?* (pp. 85–112). London: Karnac.

Carroll, R. (2009). Self-regulation: an evolving concept at the heart of body psychotherapy. In: L. Hartley, *Contemporary Body Psychotherapy: The Chiron Approach* (pp. 89–105). Abingdon: Routledge.

Cassidy, J., & Shaver, P. R. (Eds.) (1999). *Handbook of Attachment: Theory, Research, and Clinical Applications*. New York: Guilford Press.

Chiel, H. J., & Beer, R. D. (1997). The brain has a body: adaptive behavior emerges from interactions of nervous system, body and environment. *Trends in Neurosciences, 20*: 553–557.

Clarkson, P., & Mackewn, J. (1993). *Fritz Perls*. London: Sage.

Craig, A. D. (2002). How do you feel? Interoception: the sense of the physiological condition of the body. *Nature Reviews Neuroscience, 3*: 655–666.

Fogel, A. (2009). *The Psychophysiology of Self-awareness: Rediscovering the Lost Art of Body Sense*. New York: Norton.

Fonagy, P., Gergely, G., Jurist, E. J., & Target, M. (2002). *Affect Regulation, Mentalisation and the Development of the Self*. New York: Other Press.

Gallese, V. (2009). Mirror neurons, embodied simulation, and the neural basis of social identification. *Psychoanalytic Dialogues, 19*: 519–36.

Houston, G. (2003). *Brief Gestalt Therapy*. London: Sage.

Jacobs, L. (2009). Attunement and optimal responsiveness. In: R. Hycner, & L. Jacobs (Eds.), *Relational Approaches in Gestalt Therapy* (pp. 131–169). Abingdon: Routledge.

La Barre, F. (2001). *On Moving and Being Moved. Nonverbal Behaviour in Clinical Practice*. Hillsdale, NJ: Analytic Press.

Laplanche, J. (1989). *New Foundations for Psychoanalysis* (Trans. David Macey). Cambridge: Blackwell.

Llinas, R., & Churchland, P. (1997). *The Mind–brain Continuum*. New York: Carfax.

Maroda, K. J. (2010). *Psychodynamic Techniques: Working with Emotion in the Therapeutic Relationship*. New York: Guildford Press.

Mitchell, S. L. (2000). *Relationality: From Attachment to Intersubjectivity* Hillsdale, NJ: Analytic Press.

Ogden, P. (2014). Wisdom of the body, lost and found. In: K. White (Ed.), *Talking Bodies: How Do We Integrate Working with the Body in Psychotherapy from an Attachment and Relational Perspective?*, pp. 89–108. London: Karnac.

Ogden, P., Minton, K., & Pain, C. (2006). *Trauma and the Body: A Sensorimotor Approach to Psychotherapy*. New York: Norton.
Orbach, S. (2005). The psychotherapy relationship. In: J. Ryan, *How Does Psychotherapy Work?* (pp. 69–83). London: Karnac.
Orbach, S. (2010). *Bodies*. London: Profile books.
Orbach, S., & Carroll, R. (2006). Contemporary approaches to the body in psychotherapy: two psychotherapists in dialogue. In: J. Corrigall, J. Payne, & H. Wilkinson (Eds.), *About a Body: the Embodied Psychotherapist* (pp. 63–82). Hove: Brunner-Routledge.
Peters, D. (2000). Review of vibrational medicine for the twenty first century. *Caduceus*, 50: 45–46.
Porges, S. W. (2011). *The Polyvagal Theory: Neurophysiological Foundations of Emotions, Attachment, Communication, and Self-regulation*. New York: Norton.
Preston, L. (2008). The edge of awareness: Gendlin's contribution to explorations of implicit experience. *International Journal of Psychoanalytic Self Psychology*, 3(4): 347–369.
Ringstrom, P. (2001). Cultivating the improvisational in psychoanalytic treatment. *Psychoanalytic Dialogues*, 11(5): 727–754.
Schore, A. (2003). *Affect Regulation and the Repair of the Self*. New York: Norton.
Sella, Y. (2005). Recovering and eliciting precursors of meaning: a psychodynamic perspective of the body in psychotherapy. In: N. Totton (Ed.), *New Dimensions in Body Psychotherapy* (pp. 87–102). Maidenhead: Open University Press.
Soth, M. (2005). Embodied countertransference. In: N. Totton (Ed.), *New Dimensions in Body Psychotherapy* (pp. 40–55). Maidenhead: Open University Press.
Stern, D. (1985). *The Interpersonal World of the Infant: A View from Psychoanalysis and Developmental Psychology*. New York: Basic.
Target, M. (2008). Commentary. In: F. N. Busch (Ed.), *Mentalisation: Theoretical Considerations, Research Findings and Clinical Implications* (pp. 261–279). Analytic Press: New York.
Totton, N. (Ed.) (2005). *New Dimensions in Body Psychotherapy*. Maidenhead: Open University Press.
Totton, N. (2010). Wild Therapy. A talk given at the Confer Conference "The Big Idea" London, March 2010.
Trevarthen, C., & Aitken, K. J. (2001). Infant intersubjectivity: research, theory and clinical application. *Journal of Child Psychology and Psychiatry*, 42(1): 3–4.

CHAPTER THREE

Embodiment and the social bond

Nick Totton

Introduction

In recent years body psychotherapy has become a great deal better known and respected than formerly, partly because of the striking support it has received from the findings of neuroscience (Carroll, 2005–2006, 2009; Ogden, Minton & Paine, 2006; Panksepp, 2006a, b; Porges, 2011; Stauffer, 2009). Body psychotherapists have naturally repaid the favour by becoming very interested in neuroscience! More recently, though, it has sunk in that for the most part neuroscience simply confirms what we have already discovered through direct, often literally hands-on, experience. In this chapter, therefore, I shall focus on the practice and theory of body psychotherapy itself and, except in passing, refer to only a few neuroscience findings that I believe do actually clarify the picture. My goals are to develop a grounded understanding of what the often-used phrase "embodied relationship" really involves; to look at the clinical implications; and to suggest how we can move beyond the infant-focused concept of "attachment" to think instead about the nature of our social bond and our bond with the other-than-human.

Relational bodies

Let me start, then, with a quotation from Wilhelm Reich, who simultaneously created body psychotherapy as a field and, because of his radical positions, put it out of bounds for mainstream therapists for many years:

> On an elementary level, there is but one desire which issues from the biopsychic unity of the person, namely the desire to discharge inner tensions. … This is impossible without contact with the outer world. Hence, the *first* impulse of *every* creature must be the desire to establish contact with the outer world. (Reich, 1972, p. 271, original italics)

Here in a nutshell is the inherent link between the energy theories of traditional body psychotherapy, and more recent relational approaches. It is our organismic energy that needs and seeks relationship as the only way to fulfil itself.

My own brand of body psychotherapy, which I practice and teach, is called embodied-relational therapy, or ERT (Totton, 2005; Totton & Priestman, 2012, on which some parts of this chapter draw); and its name sums up what I say in the previous paragraph. ERT starts out from the perception that we are all embodied and relational beings: two core aspects of what it means to be a human. We need relationships with others to survive and thrive both physically and emotionally. As babies and infants we are totally dependent bodily on our primary caregivers; we are born, therefore, with a hardwired imperative to form relationships, to actively attract and appeal to adult humans—for example, by imitating their vocal and facial signals and rhythmically attuning to their behaviour (Hart, 2011; Stern, 1985; Trevarthen & Aitken, 2001; Wilkinson, 2010). We enter the world as bodies, primed to seek contact with other bodies. Babies can start imitating the expressions and movements of other people within minutes of birth (Meltzoff & Moore, 1995, pp. 49–50); within a similar timespan they can recognise the voice of their mother, which they have heard only from within the womb (DeCasper & Fifer, 1980; DeCasper & Spence, 1986). For years after birth our survival depends on our ability to attract and hold the attention of adult carers.

But this is an abstract way of describing what all carers for infants witness: the passionate and skilful delight babies find in creating embodied relationship, and the storms of grief and despair with which they respond to disturbances in relationship. Long before a baby can form anything describable as a thought, its bodymind is capable of complex and subtly intelligent interactions through gaze, expression, voice, and movement. We arrive in this world eager and expectant to form intense relationships, with a huge capacity to do so, which we hurl recklessly into action like a gambler or a lover staking everything on one throw of the dice. Our bodies tremble and vibrate with urgency to connect, soaring and swooping between peaks of bliss and troughs of agony and despair, visibly expanding and contracting with the responses we receive. These earliest relationships literally form and shape us and all our future relationships; throughout our lives we can experience the deepest wounding and the deepest healing in relationship. On this topic neuroscience (e.g., Gerhard, 2005; Marks-Tarlow, 2012; Schore, 2001a, b) simply confirms the long-held intuitions of body psychotherapy.

For adults as for infants, when two people meet and come together each continuously affects and conditions the experience of the other. Each relationship is unique, and develops from the conscious and unconscious reactions of both people. So in therapy, for example, each client responds differently to us, we respond differently to each of our clients, and the quality of the contact formed between us and hence of the work that we do together will to an extent be unique to that dyad.

These reactions and responses are not primarily mental events. They are sourced in *our bodily experience*, in the physiological activation set in train by the mutual impact of two people's embodiment. Much of this happens outside consciousness, and the process is too complex and extensive to track fully either from the inside or from the outside. Among its preconscious and unconscious elements are pheromonal stimulation, conveying much information about the other person's sexual and emotional status (Grammer, Fink & Neave, 2005); assessment of the other's threat capacity, determining the activity of our autonomic nervous system (ANS), the relative proportions of sympathetic and parasympathetic activation (Carroll, 2005) and activation of our social engagement system (Porges, 2011); firing of our mirror neurones in response to the other's posture, movements and verbal behaviour (Keysers, 2011; Pineda, 2010); and much more.

Although we don't generally know, and in some cases cannot know, the details of these processes, we certainly can become conscious of their final summation in our "intuitive feeling" about the other, our openness or closure, sympathy or suspicion, liking or dislike. A sizeable part of the training for any psychotherapist—though sometimes not explicitly discussed—is learning to be aware of, and to interrogate, these responses in ourselves (Marks-Tarlow, 2012). For body psychotherapists this includes picking up on our embodied responses, before or alongside their translation into an emotional response and then into psychological assessment. Many practitioners who don't identify as body psychotherapists make use of this capacity, though they are not always explicitly aware of doing so. I see this capacity to track and use one's embodied experience as the central qualification to do body psychotherapy.

Relational body psychotherapy takes this a stage further. We can conceptualise this in terms of the distinction made in psychoanalysis between a "one-body psychology" which situates problems within the analysand, and a "two-body psychology", which explores the system formed by analysand and analyst together (Aron, 1990; Balint, 1950). "Body" in this formulation derives from mathematical physics (see my discussion below); but for body psychotherapists it has a much more literal significance. In a "one-body body psychotherapy" the practitioner consults her own embodied response in order to learn about the client's issues and needs. In a "two-body body psychotherapy", however, as practitioners we *commit to* our embodied response in order to form a living, two-way relationship, which becomes the crucible of change and growth. Our body bathes in and soaks up the embodied presence of the client; we catch fire from them; we breathe them in and metabolise them; we reverberate to their rhythms, and our own rhythms shift to meet them. Out of this meeting of realities a third shared reality is born. And as I will be discussing, I sense a further development underway: a move from two bodies to a whole world full of bodies.

Somatising relationship

The specific contribution of body psychotherapy to the relational approach is to *somatise relationship*: to *flesh it out*, one might say, as part of our general commitment to supporting clients in fleshing out their whole experience of life. As James Kepner says, speaking of life in general, but in terms applicable to much therapeutic work:

> Most often, our conversation and common contact includes little of our embodied experience in its content, little reference to embodiment in gesture, and little conscious experience of ourselves or the other as embodied beings. Even when we report emotions they are rarely acknowledged as bodily events, located in our bodily self, even though one cannot experience emotion without bodily location. We keep it all very abstract with little bodily referent. It is as if our emotions had no bodily origin or location, but are something we 'thought up'. (Kepner, 2003, p. 7)

In contrast, Kepner suggests, "a body therapist must have access to their own deep embodiment and relate to the client in a deeply embodied way" (2003, p. 9): "To be deeply embodied is to have access to one's body experience as *self-experience*" (2003, p. 12, original italics).

We frequently experience a split between this "self-experience" and experience mediated through language. In Daniel Stern's view:

> Language ... causes a split in the experience of the self. It ... moves relatedness onto the impersonal, abstract level intrinsic to language and away from the personal immediate level intrinsic to ... other domains of relatedness. (Stern, 1985, pp. 162–163)

Stern is not of course arguing that language is a negative development; just that its enormous benefits come at a price of alienation from the immediacy of experience. We can sometimes perceive the languaged and the embodied aspects of experience as *opposed*, or sometimes as *complementary*; what makes the difference?

Jacques Lacan (2006) argues that therapy seeks, or should seek, to enable the production of "full" rather than "empty" speech. I suggest that what fills out "full speech" is embodiment. Deeply embodied speech is a complex modulation of the spontaneous and pleasurable breath. It has resonance, timbre, and rhythm; it emerges from chest (heart) and belly, not just from throat and mouth; in fact at its fullest it comes all the way from the feet. It is also filled out by the resonances of metaphor and imagery, which derive entirely from the physical world and largely from bodily experience. The psychoanalyst Ella Sharpe wrote that "a subterranean passage between mind and body underlies all analogy" (Sharpe, 1940, p. 202; cf. Lakoff & Johnson, 1980).

Embodied speech, in fact, occupies what Julia Kristeva (1984) calls the semiotic register, as opposed to the symbolic register of denotative meaning: it uses language as a direct expression of the body and its energies, partaking of the musicality and playfulness of vocal expression, which we find in the interaction of infant and carer. Embodied or semiotic speech is not the yardstick of some idealised state of health, but as well as the joy of self-expression bears the marks of pain, trauma and repression, the tensions imposed on the body to facilitate both the physical act of speech and other socially required behaviours. Kristeva describes the semiotic as

> a psychosomatic modality of the signifying process ... articulating ... a continuum: the connections between the (glottal and anal) sphincters in (rhythmic and intonational) vocal modulations, and those between the sphincters and family protagonists, for example. (Kristeva, 1984, pp. 28–29)

The semiotic, in other words, is the expression of character structure in speech and language; and character structure itself is the expression both of desire and of its social-familial repression. Through what we say, but even more through how we say it, we express the state and history of our embodiment, the history of our family relationships—what Katharine Young describes as "the ancestral ghost in the flesh of the present" (Young, 2002, p. 45). Young points out that our style of embodiment develops through imitation or rejection of family models of adulthood, masculinity and femininity, our judgement of how we should be:

> Out of a family repertoire of such judgements, children shape a corporeal self. Whether by imitation or resistance, their bodies memorialize the family's way of being in the world. The body is one of our family traditions. (Young, 2002, p. 26)

Hence transference needs to be understood not only as a psychological but also, and fundamentally, as a *bodily* process: a function of implicit procedural memories of childhood relationships, learnt complexes of emotional and physical response situated outside consciousness and in part repressed from consciousness. Our body learns patterns of relating in childhood and infancy, ways of positioning self in relation to the other that become an automatic part of our adult repertoire, encompassing not only embodied speech but also posture, gesture, pheromone discharge, and autonomic nervous system (ANS) activation, and extending to our basic metabolism (Eisman, 1985). To describe these ghostlike patterns of relating I am going to use the word *engram*: an old fashioned but (before it was enlisted by Scientology) respectable term for the unknown mechanism by which memory complexes are stored and then reactivated by appropriate stimulus (Lashley, 1950). In a neuroscience context, the general assumption is that these memories are stored in the brain; but I am talking about procedural memories effectively stored in the *body* (Koch, Fuchs, Summa & Muller, 2012). Without accepting any of Scientology's belief system, I appreciate its definition of the engram as "a definite and permanent trace left by a stimulus on the protoplasm of a tissue", which feels very Reichian. Embodied-relational engrams or memory complexes are enormously powerful in shaping our experience, and, equally, other people's experience of us. The therapist's countertransference is in large part an out-of-awareness reaction to the client's transference engram, and vice versa for the client: joining in the physiological dance.

To illustrate this simply, I will explore a vignette which I have used elsewhere, but will look at it in a slightly different way. Early on in therapy with a client, I found my attention drawn to their tight jaw, which seemed to express an attitude of stubborn defiance. I developed a strong wish to soften their jaw, and as soon as I felt we had established sufficient relationship I asked them whether I could press on the muscles in the angle of the jaw while encouraging them to breathe and make a noise. This didn't go at all well: the client quickly became distressed and asked me to stop, and trust between us was damaged for some while. After a few months, though, and completely forgetting the previous interaction, I did the same thing—and then again a few months later! Not surprisingly, the effect was worse each time; finally, I grasped that there was something here needing examination. The client talked about the intense physical bullying they had experienced as a child from their older brothers, and how they had felt unable to tell their parents about it: the tight jaw expressed both their inability to speak, their defiance in the face of bullying, and their holding back of tears—which were now able to be released.

But why had I acted in such a stupid and insensitive way? This enactment, it seems to me, was created by my unconsciously picking up the complex and contradictory messages embedded in my client's tight jaw, and responding to all of them at once. My bodymind knew that there was something they needed to tell me; but in trying to access it, I replicated the bullying situation itself, and drove the tears deeper within—while at the same time the situation was *showing* me, rather than *telling* me, about the original scenario. I am myself an older brother, and have my own bullying engram that was activated under cover of therapeutic helping. The client's embodied expectation of bullying and resistance cued me in to repeat my own childhood behaviour—of which, of course, I am now consciously ashamed—of enjoying physical power over someone weaker.

Many practitioners, some of them body psychotherapists and some not (e.g., Athanasiadou & Halewood, 2011; Dosamantes-Beaudry, 1997; Field, 1989; Ross, 2000; Soth, 2005; Stone, 2006; Vulcan, 2009) have observed how processes like transference, countertransference, and projection are frequently *experienced* in an embodied way by the practitioner. In fact Egan and Carr (2008) have developed a "body-centred countertransference scale" to measure the intensity of the effect, including sixteen different bodily phenomena. Booth et al. (2010) in their research on a sample of Irish clinical psychologists found the most commonly reported of these sixteen phenomena were muscle tension, sleepiness, yawning and tearfulness; the least common, but still significantly represented, were nausea, numbness, sexual arousal and genital pain. It is unsurprising that the latter group are less often reported given the greater likelihood that they will be elided from awareness.

In the model I am suggesting, transference, countertransference and projection are all bodily phenomena, based on the activation of procedural memory engrams, which are always implicit—that is, out of awareness—and often also repressed—that is, not available to awareness. The Boston Change Process Study Group refer to this as "implicit relational knowing" (Boston Change Process Study Group, 2008; Lyons-Ruth, 1998). When such engrams are active in the client, any number of channels are available for the therapist to pick them up. As Allan Schore says:

> In monitoring countertransferential responses to the patient's implicit facial, gestural, and prosodic communications, the clinician's right brain tracks at a preconscious level not only the rhythms and flows of the patient's affective states, but also the clinician's

own interoceptive bodily based affective responses to the patient's shifting arousal levels. (Schore, 2005, p. 845)

We can also include, for example, the effect of mirror neurones in creating an echo in ourselves of what we perceive happening in the other. Babette Rothschild (1993) and others have suggested that therapists' tendency to "mirror" in a more ordinary sense—deliberately or otherwise to match clients' posture, breathing, speech rhythms, etc.—renders us particularly open to this sort of echoing; as, of course, does our general position of empathic attunement.

But as I have already emphasised, all human beings are impacted on a bodily level by the feeling state of others, whether we recognise it or not, whether we welcome it or not. And the whole message of the relational turn in psychotherapy is that when the therapist is impacted by the client's transference engram, our response is outside our conscious control: our own engrams are activated, and we are swayed deeply by the infantile experiences that they encode. Both participants are then cast into a maelstrom where we struggle to survive, to self-soothe, and to recognise the actuality of the here-and-now situation and of the other. As Karen Maroda writes, once transference and countertransference appear,

> each begins to feel misunderstood by the other. They may each feel a myriad of other things, such as unloved, unappreciated, abused, or taken advantage of, by the other. Or they may defend against these negative feelings by being madly in love with each other ... emotions run high, crescendoing into overt conflict ... (Maroda, 1998, p. 4)

There is a deeper issue here, in fact. What could entitle us to make an absolute distinction between a therapist's internal experiences as traces of the client's material, and a therapist's internal experiences as traces of their own material? What would allow us to assert what Schore calls our "bodily based affective responses to the patient's shifting arousal levels" are responses, rather than events of which we should acknowledge ownership—or indeed, events to which the client's "shifting arousal levels" are responses? When two asteroids, for example, are affected by each other's gravitational fields, the difficulty of mathematically treating this mutuality other than by artificially reducing it to two separate equations, one for each body, is the original "two body problem" (Goldstein, 1980).

This is the terrain of relational therapy: a shared attempt to work through mutual feelings of distress and pain, as well as love and enjoyment. And all of its psychological complexity develops on a platform of embodied experience. It is enormously helpful in negotiating these difficult feelings to have an awareness of and openness to the bodily experience that underlies them—and at the same time, the fundamental firm and soothing quality of embodiment, the simple sway of the breath, the gurgle of the belly, the feet on the ground. Body psychotherapists have hopefully worked through their own relationship with embodiment to the extent that they can regularly find comfort in it, and endeavour to communicate this comfort to their clients.

James Kepner stresses the importance of

> the capacity of the therapist to hold [the embodied] aspect of experience as figural (bounded, central and relevant) even if, or especially if, it is not figural for the client. ... To work with embodiment ... the therapist must be able to hold a constant awareness and appreciation that the body is intrinsic to *all* human process. (Kepner, 2003, p. 9, original italics)

He says, perhaps idealistically, that "the therapist must, each hour, foster an embodied field powerful enough to support the client in holding their bodily life and experience as *intrinsic* to their ongoing experience" (Kepner, 2003, p. 10, original italics). This is certainly what we should endeavour to do; and in the context of this chapter, the importance of this "embodied field" is that it supports the client *and the therapist* in contacting the embodied ground on which their complex and difficult feelings and fantasies about each other have been erected.

Embodied relating beyond the therapeutic dyad

Embodied relating happens, of course, not only in the therapy room, and not even only between human beings. There is a constant interplay between our relationship with other people, our relationship with our own bodymind experience, and our relationship with the world itself and all the other-than-human and more-than-human entities that exist there. Diminished contact with our own embodiment accompanies and is accompanied by diminished delight in and love for the world we inhabit, and diminished empathy for the suffering of other beings.

So as an embodied-relational therapist, my endeavour, in the therapy room and in life generally, is for a free relationality in all three dimensions: contact with my proprioceptive and kinesthetic awareness and with my embodied emotions; contact with my environment and how it impacts on my well-being; and contact with other people, using all the specialised sensitivities with which we have evolved. Reich's case histories give marvellous descriptions of how these three dimensions interact to form a solid whole. More than once, he describes a client discovering through body psychotherapy a profound relationship with the cosmos:

> In the process of working through this connection, his personality underwent a conspicuous change. His superficiality disappeared; he became serious. The seriousness appeared very suddenly during one of the sessions. The patient said literally: 'I don't understand; everything has become so deadly serious all of a sudden.' (Reich, 1983, p. 321)

As his body continues to surrender more deeply to energy flow, the patient recovers a memory from about two years old:

> He was alone with his mother at a summer resort. It was a clear starry night. His mother was asleep and breathing deeply; outside he could hear the steady pounding of the waves on the beach. The mood he had felt then was the same deeply serious, somewhat sad and melancholy mood which he experienced now. We can say that he remembered one of the situations from earliest childhood in which he had still allowed himself to experience his vegetative (orgastic) longing. (Reich, 1983, pp. 324–325)

In ERT we speak of "wild mind", and of the "wild therapy" that follows from its recognition (Totton, 2011): we can flexibly listen to and learn from body sensations, dreams, intuition, free association, the activity of clouds, birds and animals, alongside our powers of thinking and reasoning. To live in wild mind is to acknowledge the rich intelligence of the non-rational parts of myself and of the world around me. Surrendering to and trusting these messy, seemingly chaotic kinds of knowing brings a profound experience of support and release from having to hold it all together and have all the answers. It depends, at least partially, on our capacity for secure attachment. I am thinking, though, of a very different kind of secure attachment from that available in contemporary Western society: one which is not a function of the isolated mother–child dyad, but is held within and inseparable from the wider social bond. To explain what I mean I am going to take a detour through hunter-gatherer societies (summarising fuller discussions in Totton, 2011).

Writing about the world view of hunter-gatherer cultures, Guy Barker says:

> Commonly the environment is regarded as a benign spiritual home ... relations with it are modelled on the same principle of sharing that applies within the human community: it is the source of all good things, 'a giving environment' ... Foragers ... commonly do not have words for distinguishing between people, animals and plants as separate categories ... (Barker, 2006, pp. 58–59)

Barker is describing a culture that *includes rather than excludes*. It includes the other-than-human within the same system of knowledge and relationship as the human; and it models both these communities as essentially generous, essentially sharing. It is able to do this because it doesn't seek to *own* the world, but only to live within it, to pass through it: humans belong to the land, not the land to humans. And this relationship with the world both allows and requires humans to understand what happens where they live, and to persuade and encourage the world to satisfy their needs.

How are these attitudes developed? For foragers to survive they must cooperate and share. For children to survive and reach adulthood they must be constantly supported by grown-ups. Infants in forager cultures are held and carried at all times—not only by mothers, but by relatives and allies of many kinds (Hrdy, 2009, pp. 73–82; Sorenson, 1998, pp. 83–84). To grow up in this way—cherished and nurtured by all around you—is to directly experience the world as "a giving environment"; and this upbringing facilitates the development of an ecological self, a wild mind.

Sarah Blaffer Hrdy (2009) highlights how the Neolithic shift to sedentary agricultural society degraded child-rearing; she identifies two aspects of forager society that while in some ways problematic lead to good nurturing. In most forager cultures, the relative shortage of high-grade nutrition means that the average age of menstruation is sixteen. It also means that mothers need to devote considerable time to their own survival needs, making it impossible for them to look after children by themselves: successful child-rearing is necessarily a collective enterprise involving at the very least grandmothers, and often many more group members. The hard fact is that in this environment poorly parented children don't grow up at all.

By contrast, in agricultural society, because of a relative abundance of high-grade protein the age of puberty steeply declines, and also more infants survive; but the shift to patrilocal and patriarchal structures also means that younger mothers have less support from their own mothers and other kinswomen—as well as increasingly removing fathers from the "women's work" of childcare (Hrdy, 2009, pp. 287–288). These factors, combined with the rise of competitive, dominance-based structures, set up a context for insecure and disorganised attachment, leading to potentially even worse child-rearing in the next generation.

> The end of the Pleistocene marked a consequential divide in the way children were raised as people began to settle in one place, build walled houses, grow and store food. ... Child survival became increasingly decoupled from the need to be in constant physical contact with another person, or surrounded by responsive, protective caretakers in order to pull through. ... After the Pleistocene, and increasingly over the ensuing centuries, even young women still psychologically immature and woefully lacking in sympathy or social support could nevertheless be well-fed enough to ovulate and conceive while still in their early teens. (Hrdy, 2009, pp. 286–287)

It is fair to say that many of the problems we deal with every day in therapy have their origins in this Neolithic bargain. Both infant attachment and the social bond were transformed by the social and economic changes that took place. The newly degraded status of women, together with the increased possibility of survival for poorly reared children, gave rise to insecure and disorganised attachment patterns, which must have been previously rare or unknown—as I have said, in

Pleistocene forager bands any infant who survived would necessarily be securely attached (Hrdy, 2009, p. 290). This in turn created disturbed and dangerous adults whose aggression and need for dependency was harnessed by the newly arising state, as continues to happen in every army up to the present. The social bond, partly influenced by these new attachment patterns, shifted from a free partnership of equals to a patriarchal hierarchy underwritten by theism, a state of affairs psychically damaging to every man, woman, and child. These changes are the psychic equivalent of asteroid strikes; their effects are still with us.

What would a therapist from a forager culture, if we can imagine such a person, make of us and our problems? Well, we know that shamans, the nearest equivalent figures, are not too impressed. Much of what we encounter in the therapy room is trauma created by the child-rearing environment of the patriarchal nuclear family—an environment that therapy in general and attachment theory in particular tend to treat as natural and innate. The sort of secure attachment that is the optimum outcome of such child-rearing can alternatively be seen as an obsessive and fragile dependence on a single, almost always female, carer. And the sort of "autonomous" adult ego that develops from this experience is one suited to and, with luck, equipped to survive in a society based on relationships of dominance and competition. However, to fully support and justify this position would take another chapter.

Moving from attachment to social bonding

This is where I want to bring in one piece of neuroscience that I do feel actively illuminates body psychotherapy: the polyvagal theory developed by Stephen Porges (2011). This is a recent theory that may or may not stand up scientifically over time, but as *imagery* I think it has enormous force and conviction and fits totally with the experience of body psychotherapy. It's a new interpretation of the autonomic nervous system that focuses on one part of the parasympathetic side of the autonomic system. The parasympathetic is basically about calming and soothing and relaxing, whereas the sympathetic side is about activating and waking up. It's much more complicated than that, but this simple picture is certainly not wrong, just simple.

Porges looks at one branch of a cranial nerve called the vagal nerve, a major part of the parasympathetic system. The branch on which he focuses works to calm and relax the heart. (The other branch functions similarly with the guts.) He shows that, although the vagal system is primarily about calming things down, this branch of it can actually be used as a flexible and controllable way to rapidly stimulate the heart and the metabolism in general, by *lessening* its effect: if the vagal nerve is *less* activated, the heart will be *more* active. This offers a much more flexible and less earth-shaking alternative to the sympathetic system's adrenalin-based way of activating the metabolism: a system that can be easily ramped up and down without flooding us with adrenalin and leaving us exhausted.

So the vagal nerve provides a way of energising ourselves to act in the world while not entering into survival mode, fight-flight ways of processing events. In other words, it is a precise tool for social interaction. Instead of an on-off switch, it is adjustable, like a tap: we can have precisely the level of activation appropriate to the situation, and adjust this as the situation changes. Under normal circumstances, the sympathetic will only get activated if this vagal system is not working properly—like using a sledgehammer to crack a nut because the nutcrackers are broken.

Porges points out that this branch of the vagal nerve is one of several cranial nerves that all originate in the same area of the brain, an area that in our early aquatic ancestors was concerned with the function of the gills. If we put together the operation of all these cranial nerves, we get a very interesting picture. Some of them are still concerned with breath, and also with sucking, swallowing, salivation, and vocalisation—in other words, with all the mechanisms that allow first of all breast feeding without suffocation, and then eventually articulate speech. Others let us tense the muscles of the middle ear, creating the ability to pick out and discriminate the frequencies of speech from the hum of background noise. Others control the expressive muscles of the face, and the muscles of the eyelids, influencing eye contact. All in all, this is an elaborate and subtle system for interrelating with other people, first as infants and then as adults: a system developed over evolutionary time by co-opting and synthesising pre-existing anatomy and physiology for new purposes. This sort of process is known as "exaptation"—using a feature that evolved for one purpose to do something else altogether.

So, Porges is describing a complex interactive network of cranial nerves and functional systems that was originally concerned with absorbing oxygen from water; gradually developed in mammals into a system for absorbing food and comfort from the mother's breast; and then, in humans, brought this together with visual and vocal interaction with our carer, becoming in adults a system for absorbing relational nourishment from our social context. And what is particularly pleasing for me as a body psychotherapist is that the whole system—what Porges calls the social engagement system—is focused on the *heart*, on the ability of good, nourishing relating to calm and soften the heart. The theory offers neuroscientific backing for the experience of *heart to heart contact*.

It also fleshes out and makes concrete the body psychotherapy concept of *facing* (Boadella, 1987), one of a triad that also includes *grounding* and *centring*. David Boadella writes:

> Facing is concerned with recognition, with how we see people, with the qualities of lumination that develop when people really face each other. Clear seeing between people … encourages deeper being. (Boadella, 1987, p. 113)

He goes on immediately to discuss *sounding*, the role of speech and voice.

The social engagement system, then, is where many of our embodied-relational engrams are created and stored. Porges' theory is only one of several ways in which current neuroscience says that we are born ready to go, socially speaking: that our social, relational energy is *bodily* energy—after all, what else could it be? and that this energy needs to be plugged into a live relationship in order to develop. If this doesn't happen well—either for internal reasons, or if our carers fail to meet us in the dance of social engagement—then the body falls back on cruder, earlier, less subtly adjustable systems of activation, based on the sympathetic nervous system's binary, fight-flight approach, flooding itself with adrenalin, or on the parasympathetic strategies of immobility and dissociation. An extreme response to things going wrong with the social engagement system, Porges suggests, is autism. Less extreme responses might be shyness, boringness, shame, or aggression. And there will also be specific situational responses to specific stimuli—what I am calling relational engrams.

An important aspect of the social engagement system theory is its focus on the biological conditions that allow human social bonding. As Porges says, drawing on the work of his partner Sue Carter (2005), social behaviors associated with nursing, reproduction, and the formation of strong pair bonds require a unique biobehavioral state characterized by immobilization without fear, and immobilization without fear is mediated by a co-opting of the neural circuit regulating defensive freezing behaviors through the involvement of oxytocin. (Porges, 2005, p. 33)

Again, Porges is discussing a process of "exaptation": a parasympathetic system for defensive freezing has been developed into a way to relax and stay in contact even under strong stimulus—something of obvious relevance to psychotherapy. One of the things that attracts me about the social engagement system theory is that it represents a move on from attachment theory, with its focus on mother–infant relationships, to a theory of *social bonding*, of adult-adult relationship, which builds on infant attachment but transforms it into a peer interaction.

Traditionally, psychotherapy has focused on the attachment dyad and the autonomous individual ego as the two sides of the therapy coin. I believe that it is time for us to consider other modes of subjectivity and relationality, in particular modes that emphasise the collective and transpersonal. It will always be a crucial part of our job to elicit and explore infant relational engrams, which impact on clients' capacity for here and now relating. But perhaps we need to move back a little towards Freud's original view of transference as an *obstacle* to therapy rather than its primary *modus operandi* (Bollas, 2007). Certainly I would like us to stop seeing the therapeutic relationship as inherently one between child and parent, and seeing this as the agent of cure rather than as what needs to be cured. Rather than re-parenting, I would like us to think more in terms of *de*-parenting: progressing to a point where both client and therapist can recognise that there are no parents and no babies in the room. I know that I am being one-sided in this emphasis: my intention is to rebalance what is currently a highly unbalanced approach.

The ERT approach to therapeutic relating

I want to come back now to what embodied-relational therapy places at the centre of its work: the project of offering and modelling embodiment to and for our clients. The more we attend to our embodiment—the better we are at grounding, centring, and facing—the more able we are to relate effectively—and many of the problems our clients bring are bound up with issues of embodiment.

How can we offer and model embodiment—and what do we mean by embodiment? Body psychotherapists use "embodiment" as a name for the moment-by-moment experience of our existence as living bodies, with all the joy and grief, pleasure and pain, power and vulnerability that involves. Embodiment is not a *state*, not an either/or deal, something to be achieved as a finality, but an ongoing *process of becoming embodied* and more and more deeply committed to our corporeal experience: an exploration of and dialogue with the organismic aspect of our being without which we cannot exist but which we always have difficulty fully accepting (Totton, 2008). It challenges us to own and integrate the various woundings we encounter in life, rather than leaving them frozen in patterns of bodily tension and avoidance, which create a numb spot in our awareness and sensitivity. The reality for each individual will always be a set of compromises, as our embodiment finds ways to make the best of its situation to preserve as much freedom and flexibility as possible; and body psychotherapy tries to help clients explore and re-evaluate these bodily choices.

Our lived awareness of being bodies encompasses the bodily process of absorbing and enacting social and cultural reality. From this point of view, embodiment is a summation of how the body suffers, accommodates, and transmits an ensemble of social and cultural stresses and tensions, which often therefore appear as simply "the way things are". Embodiment in this sense can often suppress embodiment in the other sense, substituting an objectified perception of the body. In a culture largely alienated from embodied experience, there is an ongoing struggle between lived embodiment and the body as object, in which body psychotherapy has always been deeply involved. As Don Hanlon Johnson says:

> Underlying the various techniques and schools, one finds a desire to regain an intimate connect with bodily processes: breath, movement impulses, balance and sensibility. In that shared impulse, this community is best understood within a much broader movement of resistance to the West's long history of denigrating the value of the human body and the natural environment. (Johnson, 1995, p. xvi)

When we as therapists are impacted by the client's embodiment, we directly experience in our embodied countertransference its compromises, its contradictions, how it is incorporated (literally!) into social narratives and also resists or evades such incorporation—all of this, for the length of the session, becomes part of our own lived embodiment, and resonates with our own multiplicity of compromises and contradictions.

It is crucial to acknowledge our own defences against embodied relationship. To engage in this way makes us very vulnerable, it moves us into a state of "liminal awareness" (Bernstein, 2005; Totton, 2011) where we are in a sense at the mercy of the other's feelings. Sometimes, as therapists, we will just not be up for this; sometimes the client will be more embodied than us, more relational than us—and sometimes we will experience this as an intolerable demand to which we react with coldness and distance, or even disguised aggression. None of this is catastrophic so long as we can allow it into awareness—even when the client notices it first!—and explore, with the client, what is happening for us and why, and what needs to be done about it.

For this style of therapy we need to make ourselves available for our clients to relate to us, meeting them where they are and in the channels they find comfortable. People have very different styles of making contact, and we need to be versatile and flexible enough to have many different contact styles in our repertoire. We also need to allow ourselves to be moved in the sense of being *moved around*—to be available to receive the fantasies, emotional responses and relational behaviours of our clients. A lot of our work involves witnessing how our clients relate to us, and witnessing our embodied response—which may in fact be the main way we become aware of what they are doing. Asking ourselves, "What's happening to me as I sit with this client?" "What shape is this client pushing me into?"

Working with the relationship is challenging, a subtle balance of committing to the relationship, and stepping outside it to witness what's unfolding—a continual challenge not to identify with and act from your experience with this client in an unconsidered way. To an extent, this is impossible—another of the paradoxes of therapy. Staying with this tension around our reaction to our clients and how much we can and can't inhibit our response is central to working relationally.

We can feel pushed, seduced, lured, lulled, charmed, hustled, ambushed, and challenged into certain shapes by our clients. Often the shape feels familiar, since there has to be a "receptor site" in us that responds to the client's cue: sometimes a shape that we like—the helpful, compassionate, accepting therapist or the intelligent, knowledgeable, experienced practitioner—or sometimes one we don't like so much: the judge, the parent, the impatient, tired, imperfect human being. Other shapes we find ourselves in are more unusual for us, more stretching, perhaps illuminating adventures. We need at times to be able to support our clients in moving us into shapes that we don't like or don't know, and to allow them to take up shapes that they don't like or don't know. Each of us has a different set of behaviours and emotions that we find difficult to support in ourselves and others; and we need to know what these are. Feeling ourselves experiencing or receiving anger, hatred, mistrust, seduction, uncertainty, can be very hard.

When we get pushed out of shape we are challenged to hold on to our sense of being good enough as a therapist. Sometimes it can be hard not to collapse into what it seems our clients are saying about us; that we're failing them, misunderstanding them. When we begin to get lost in such thoughts it's good to remind ourselves that this is part of the territory, and therapeutically valuable *whether or not it is accurate*. Whatever the regulators say, therapy is an intrinsically risky undertaking that cannot be made wholly safe if it is to be effective; and this is one of the areas where riskiness becomes foregrounded. Very often, the trauma from which our client has been suffering can only be fully brought into the therapy by being re-enacted there, as in my earlier example.

Conclusion

Whatever resources of expertise we bring to bear on body psychotherapy, drawing either from neuroscience or from other forms of skill and knowledge, it remains still and always an interpersonal, intersubjective process. Our great contribution to psychotherapy as a whole is our profound sense of how *embodied* intersubjectivity really is—and of how a person's style of embodiment defines their style of intersubjectivity, and vice versa.

In this chapter I have argued and tried to demonstrate that embodiment and relationship are inseparable, both in human existence and in the practice of body psychotherapy. If we explore embodiment, we encounter relationship; if we explore relationship, we encounter embodiment. Effective therapeutic work depends on being able to recognise the constant interplay between these two aspects of being human, and follow and support the shifts of charge from one to the other.

References

Aron, L. (1990). One person and two person psychologies and the method of psychoanalysis. *Psychoanalytic Psychology, 7*(4): 475–485.

Athanasiadou, C., & Halewood, A. (2011). A grounded theory exploration of therapists' experiences of somatic phenomena in the countertransference. *European Journal of Psychotherapy & Counselling, 13*(3): 247–262.

Balint, M. (1950). Changing therapeutical aims and techniques in psychoanalysis. *International Journal of Psycho-Analysis, 31*: 117–124.

Barker, G. (2006). *The Agricultural Revolution in Prehistory: Why Did Foragers Become Farmers?* Oxford: Oxford University Press.

Bernstein, J. (2005). *Living in the Borderland*. London: Routledge.

Boadella, D. (1987). *Lifestreams: An Introduction to Biosynthesis*. London: Routledge & Kegan Paul.

Bollas, C. (2007). *The Freudian Moment*. London: Karnac.

Booth, A., Trimble, T., & Egan, J. (2010). Body-centred counter-transference in a sample of Irish clinical psychologists. *Irish Psychologist, 36*(12): 284–289.

Boston Change Process Study Group (2008). Forms of relational meaning: issues in the relations between the implicit and reflective-verbal domains. *Psychoanalytic Dialogues, 18*: 125–148.

Carroll, R. (2005). Neuroscience and 'the law of the self': the autonomic nervous system updated, re-mapped and in relationship. In: N. Totton (Ed.), *New Dimensions in Body Psychotherapy* (pp. 13–29). Maidenhead: Open University Press.

Carroll, R. (2006). A new era for psychotherapy: Panksepp's affect model in the context of neuroscience and its implications for contemporary psychotherapy practice. In: J. Corrigal, H. Payne, & H. Wilkinson (Eds.), *About A Body: Working with the Embodied Mind in Psychotherapy* (pp. 50–62). Hove: Routledge.

Carroll, R. (2009). Self-regulation—an evolving concept at the heart of body psychotherapy. In: L. Hartley (Ed.), *Contemporary Body Psychotherapy: The Chiron Approach* (pp. 89–105). Hove: Routledge.

Carter, S. (2005). Biological perspectives on social attachment and bonding. In: C. S. Carter, L. Ahnert, K. E. Grossman, S. B. Hrdy, M. E. Lamb,

S. W. Porges, & N. Sachser (Eds.), *Attachment and Bonding: A New Synthesis*, (pp. 85–100). Cambridge, MA: MIT Press.

DeCasper, A. J., & Fifer, W. P. (1980). Of human bonding: newborns prefer their mothers' voices. *Science, 208*: 1174–1176.

DeCasper, A. J., & Spence, M. J. (1986). Prenatal maternal speech influences newborns' perception of speech sounds. *Infant Behavior and Development, 9*: 133–150.

Dosamantes-Beaudry, I. (1997). Revisioning dance/movement therapy. *American Journal of Dance Therapy, 19*(1): 16–23.

Egan, J., & Carr, A. (2008). Body-centred countertransference in female trauma therapists. *Irish Association of Counselling and Psychotherapy Quarterly Journal, 8*: 24–27.

Eisman, J. (1985). Character typologies. In: R. Kurtz, Hakomi Therapy (pp. 1–19). Boulder, Colorado: Hakomi Institute.

Field, N. (1989). Listening with the body: An exploration in the counter-transference. *British Journal of Psychotherapy, 5*(40): 512–522.

Gerhard, S. (2004). *Why Love Matters: How Affection Shapes a Baby's Brain*. London: Routledge.

Goldstein, H. (1980). *Classical Mechanics* (2nd edn.). New York: Addison-Wesley.

Grammer, K., Fink, B., & Neave, N. (2005). Human pheromones and sexual attraction. *European Journal of Obstetrics & Gynecology and Reproductive Biology, 118*(2): 135–142.

Hart, S. (2011). *The Impact of Attachment*. New York: Norton.

Hrdy, S. B. (2009). *Mothers and Others: The Evolutionary Origins of Mutual Understanding*. London: Belknap.

Johnson, D. H. (1997). Introduction. In: D. H. Johnson (Ed.), *Bone, Breath and Gesture: Practices of Embodiment*, (pp. ix–xviii). Berkeley, CA: North Atlantic Books.

Kepner, J. (2003). The embodied field. *British Gestalt Journal, 12*(1): 6–14.

Keysers, C. (2011). *The Empathic Brain*. Groningen: Social Brain Press.

Koch, S. C., Fuchs, T., Summa, M. & Muller, C. (Eds.) (2012). *Body Memory, Metaphor and Movement*. Amsterdam: John Benjamins.

Kristeva, J. (1984). *Revolution in Poetic Language*. New York: Columbia University Press.

Lacan, J. (2006 [1953]). The function and field of speech and language in psychoanalysis. In: B. Fink (Trans.), *Ecrits*, (pp. 196–268). New York: Norton.

Lakoff, G., & Johnson, M. (1980). *Metaphors We Live By*. Chicago: University of Chicago Press.

Lashley, K. (1950). In search of the engram. *Society of Experimental Biology, Symposium, 4*: 454–482.

Lyons-Ruth, K. (1998). Implicit relational knowing: its role in development and psychoanalytic treatment. *Infant Mental Health Journal*, 19(3): 282–289.

Marks-Tarlow, T. (2012). *Clinical Intuition in Psychotherapy: The Neurobiology of Embodied Response.* New York: Norton.

Maroda, K. (2002). *Seduction, Surrender, and Transformation: Emotional Engagement in the Analytic Process.* London: Psychology Press.

Meltzoff, A. N., & Moore, M. K. (1995). Infants' understanding of people and things: From body imitation to folk psychology. In: J. L. Bermudez, A. Marcel, & N. Eilan (Eds.), *The Body and the Self* (pp. 43–69). Cambridge, MA: MIT Press.

Ogden, P., Minton, K., & Paine, C. (2006). *Trauma and the Body: A Sensorimotor Approach to Psychotherapy.* New York: Norton.

Panksepp, J. (2004). *Affective Neuroscience: The Foundations of Human and Animal Emotions.* Oxford: Oxford University Press.

Panksepp, J. (2006). The core emotional systems of the mammalian brain: The fundamental substrates of human emotions. In: J. Corrigal, H. Payne, & H. Wilkinson (Eds.), *About a Body: Working with the Embodied Mind in Psychotherapy* (pp. 14–32). Hove: Routledge.

Pineda, J. A. (Ed.) (2010). *Mirror Neuron Systems.* Valley Stream, NY: Humana Press.

Porges, S. W. (2005). The role of social engagement in attachment and bonding: a phylogenetic perspective. In: C. S. Carter, L. Ahnert, K. E. Grossman, S. B. Hrdy, M. E. Lamb, S. W. Porges, & N. Sachser (Eds.), *Attachment and Bonding: A New Synthesis*, (pp. 33–54). Cambridge, MA: MIT Press.

Porges, S. W. (2011). *The Polyvagal Theory: Neurophysiological Foundations of Emotions, Attachment, Communication, and Self-Regulation.* New York: Norton.

Reich, W. (1972 [1945]). *Character Analysis.* New York: Farrar, Straus & Giroux.

Reich, W. (1983 [1942]). *The Function of the Orgasm.* London: Souvenir Press.

Ross, M. (2000). Body talk: somatic countertransference. *Psychodynamic Counselling*, 6(4): 451–467.

Rothschild, B. (1994). Transference & countertransference: a common sense perspective. *Energy and Character*, 25(2): 8–12.

Schore, A. N. (2000a). The effects of a secure attachment relationship on right brain development, affect regulation, and infant mental health. *Infant Mental Health Journal*, 22(1–2): 7–66.

Schore, A. N. (2000b). The effects of early relational trauma on right brain development, affect regulation, and infant mental health. *Infant Mental Health Journal*, 22(1–2): 201–269.

Schore, A. (2005). A neuropsychoanalytic viewpoint. Commentary on a paper by Steven H. Knoblauch. *Psychoanalytic Dialogues*, 15(6): 829–854.

Sharpe, E. F. (1940). Psycho-physical problems revealed in language: an examination of metaphor. *International Journal of Psycho-Analysis*, 21: 201–213.

Sorenson, E. R. (1998). Preconquest consciousness. In: H. Wautischer (Ed.), *Tribal Epistemologies: Essays in the Philosophy of Anthropology* (pp. 79–113). Aldershot: Ashgate Publishing.

Soth, M. (2005). Embodied countertransference. In: N. Totton (Ed.), *New Dimensions in Body Psychotherapy* (pp. 40–55). Maidenhead: Open University Press.

Stauffer, K. (2009). The use of neuroscience in body psychotherapy: theoretical and clinically relevant aspects. In: L. Hartley (Ed.), *Contemporary Body Psychotherapy: The Chiron Approach* (pp. 138–150). Hove: Routledge.

Stern, D. (1985). *The Interpersonal World of the Infant*. New York: Basic.

Stone, M. (2006). The analyst's body as tuning fork: embodied resonance in countertransference. *Journal of Analytical Psychology*, 51(1): 109–124.

Totton, N. (2005). Embodied-Relational Therapy. In: N. Totton (Ed.), *New Dimensions in Body Psychotherapy* (pp. 168–181). Maidenhead: Open University Press.

Totton, N. (2009). Body psychotherapy and social theory. *Body, Movement and Dance in Psychotherapy*, 4(3): 187–200.

Totton, N. (2011). *Wild Therapy*. Ross-on-Wye: PCCS.

Totton, N., & Priestman, A. (2012). Embodiment and relationship: two halves of one whole. In: C. Young (Ed.), *About Relational Body Psychotherapy* (pp. 35–68). Stow, Galashiels: Body Psychotherapy Publications.

Trevarthen, C., & Aitken, K. J. (2001). Infant intersubjectivity: research, theory and clinical applications. *Journal of Child Psychology and Psychiatry*, 42(1): 3–48.

Vulcan, M. (2009). Is there any body out there?: A survey of literature on somatic countertransference and its significance for DMT. *The Arts in Psychotherapy*, 36: 275–281.

Wilkinson, M. (2010). *Changing Minds in Therapy: Emotion, Attachment, Trauma, and Neurobiology*. New York: Norton.

Young, K. (2002). The memory of the flesh: the family body in somatic psychology. *Body & Society*, 8(3): 25–47.

CHAPTER FOUR

Attachment and energy psychology: explorations at the interface of bodily, mental, relational, and transpersonal aspects of human behaviour and experience

Phil Mollon

In recent years, the field of energy psychology has opened up hitherto unimaginable realms of psychotherapeutic healing of astonishing depth and speed. The claims of unusual success, by enthusiastic pioneers and "early adopters" have been fully vindicated as research has accumulated.

So what is energy psychology (or EP, to which it is often abbreviated)? It is a family of therapeutic methods that involve (1) tapping or holding acupressure meridian, or chakra energy centres, whilst (2) the client thinks of a target troublesome thought or memory. In doing this, the emotional distress is dissipated (provided the internal objections to resolving the distress have been addressed). Practitioners and clients find that these approaches, when used with knowledge and skill, are rapid, non-distressing, and can address deeper issues than talk-based therapy.

Some common versions include: thought field therapy (TFT); emotional freedom techniques (EFT); tapas acupressure technique (TAT); advanced integrative therapy (AIT)—and my own approach—psychoanalytic energy psychotherapy (PEP). The lineage developed originally from the work of chiropractor George Goodheart in the

1960s, in Detroit, and psychiatrist Dr John Diamond, who studied with Goodheart.

In 1998, the Association for Comprehensive Energy Psychology was formed, providing a professional home, code of ethics, certification, and scientific conferences. A growing body of evidence supports these methods.

The subtle energy system and its use in EP

Most of the EP modalities involve somehow stimulating the body's subtle energy system, usually the meridians or chakras, whilst a troubling thought, emotion, experience, or memory is held in mind. But what is the body's energy system? Our scientific understanding of it is rudimentary, but we have found ways of working therapeutically with this energetic anatomy. Many strange features have been described, anomalous to conventional science. These cannot be explained satisfactorily by quantum mechanics (Tiller, 2007), despite popular allusions to these. The best overall text is *Life Force, The Scientific Basis* by physicist Claude Swanson (2010).

Here he states:

> Every cell in the body has the basic molecular machinery to be any kind of cell. The actions of the DNA tell it to specialise into the type of cell needed in any location in the body, forming a liver cell, or a hair cell, for example… The holographic field around and within the body provides the blueprint which governs this. It tells the DNA in each cell, based on its location within the pattern, how it should specialise. This is an enormously important discovery which has only unfolded in the last few years … Biophotons form an important part of this picture … quantized packets of light generated by the DNA and other large molecules … (Swanson, 2010, p. 186)

He describes how coherent light from the DNA, travelling to other cells, vibrating in step with each other, create an interference pattern—a hologram—"a three dimensional pattern of energy which serves as the template of the body" (p. 186). It is the acupuncture meridians that carry these signals throughout the body and regulate the form and function of the organism.

> Recent research indicates that acupuncture meridians are universal. They play an essential role in the growth and regulation of all life forms. In the growing egg they develop before other organs. (Swanson, 2010, p. 139)

The meridians appear to function as the step-down bridge between the higher dimensional energy body and the physical body.

> The acupuncture meridian system seems to serve as the 'backbone' along which signals pass, enabling cells and organs to communicate. It helps produce and maintain a coherent holographic pattern which guides growth and healing … the acupuncture system is the bridge between the subtle world of Qi, energy healing, Reiki and Qigong, on the one hand, and the physiological world of the organs and cells. (p. 140)

Swanson describes how the meridians can be tracked by radioactive tracers and acoustic imagery. They carry a fluid rich in RNA and DNA and stem cells, and are lines of lowered electrical resistance, transmitting holographic imagery and generating "torsion fields" outside the body. The holographic energy fields communicate both within the body and outside the body. Thus, each of us is a communicative energy field, embedded in a matrix of energy fields, continually receiving and transmitting information with other energy fields.

Despite their variety of clinical procedures, EP methods all seem to manage to engage the mind and the body's energy system concurrently, thereby creating a therapeutic synergy that allows psychological (and associated physiological) change at a speed and depth hitherto regarded as impossible. Many have discovered *how* to do this, but we do not really know *why* this works.

What happens when these procedures are used it that the distress initially felt is no longer there by the end of the session—for example, people will say, "I can't think about it anymore" or "I can think about it but it no longer bothers me in the same way". Painful emotions and bodily sensations may be activated briefly, but are soon discharged.

Where there has been extensive abuse, trauma, or prolonged stress, the "emotions in the body" may be intense—may move *up the body* in sensations of wanting to vomit or scream, or *down the body* in sensations of wanting to defecate. The amount of emotion held in the body can be astonishing to witness.

Where the meridian and chakra system is partially blocked, energy "tapping" will not lead to resolution of distress and might be experienced as unpleasant.

Research evidence

Is there objective research evidence to support reports made by enthusiasts for EP? Clinical psychologist David Feinstein, in an updated review of research on EP (Feinstein, 2012), notes that early claims of unusual results for energy psychology methods—in terms of speed, durability, and range of application—evoked scepticism. Critics argued the reported results were improbable and purported mechanisms implausible. However, as research has become more rigorous and sophisticated, results have vindicated these original claims. No study has disconfirmed these results.

Feinstein found forty-nine studies that (1) involved acupoint tapping, (2) presented clinical outcome data, (3) were peer reviewed. Seventeen of these were randomised controlled trials. Here are some examples:

Church, Yount, and Brooks (2012)

Eighty-three participants. Three groups: (1) an hour of EFT; (2) an hour of talk therapy; (3) no treatment.

The group who received an hour of EFT showed a 24% drop in cortisol levels, whilst the other two groups showed no drop.

The EFT group also showed greater improvement in subjective feelings or anxiety and depression, as measured by the SA-45 (Symptom Assessment-45 Questionnaire).

Fang et al. (2009)

A ten-year research programme at Harvard Medical School has used brain imaging studies to show that stimulation of specific acupuncture points caused significant decreases in activity in the amygdala, hippocampus, and other parts of the limbic system associated with fear.

Four recent randomised controlled trials

Connolly and Sakai (2011)

145 survivors of Rwandan genocide. Single session of TFT *vs.* wait list control.

Pre-post test scores on two standardised measures of PTSD showed decreases at 0.001 level of significance—sustained at two-year follow up.

Church, Piña, Reategui, and Brooks (2012)

Sixteen abused male adolescents with PTSD. Single EFT session *vs.* wait list control.

All eight in the treatment group no longer met the criteria for PTSD after the single EFT session—thirty days after treatment.

Karatzias et al. (2011)

Participants were allowed up to eight sessions of EFT. The outcomes were positive, with voluntary termination after average 3.8 sessions.

Church et al. (2013)

Eighty-four military veterans with PTSD—assigned to six sessions of EFT or wait list control (subsequently given treatment). All participants no longer met the criteria for PTSD following EFT.

There are many other studies of EP that are not randomised controlled trials.

Studies have shown EP to be effective also in relation to:

Specific anxieties and phobias
Generalised anxiety
Depression
Pain and physical illness
Performance anxiety
Weight control
Athletic performance.

Traditional psychotherapy has tended to neglect the body

It can be argued (Mollon, 2005a) that Freud and particularly his later student Wilhelm Reich were energy psychologists—Freud using the term "libido" and Reich "orgone". Strachey (1962, p. 63) described

Freud's theory of a quasi-electrical energy as "the most fundamental of all his hypotheses".

Freud's referred to:

> a quota of affect or sum of excitation—which possesses all the characteristics of a quantity ... which is capable of increase, diminution, displacement and discharge, and which is spread over the memory traces of ideas somewhat as an electrical charge is spread over the surface of the body ... (Freud, 1894, pp. 60–61)

This is startlingly close to contemporary findings within the field of energy psychology, where the flow or blockage of the body's bioelectrical energy system, as it expresses the dynamics of the psyche, is a crucial aspect of our emotional experience.

Psychoanalysis abandoned the energy concept, and Reich was disparaged as insane in his reports of orgone (Reich, 1942), because these phenomena could not then be integrated into other areas of scientific understanding. Energy psychology represents a rediscovery of the energy concept. The body itself has been neglected in much of the psychotherapeutic and psychological literature—creating a discourse that appeared to address a disembodied mind. By contrast, Freud's own early patients showed disturbances in their bodily functions (hysteria), and he formulated their problems in terms of the body-based libido, with its progression through a series of bodily zones. In his well-known phrase, he stated that the ego is "first and foremost a body ego" (1923, p. 25).

Trauma is obviously very much a bodily as well as a mental event, with extreme physiological and brain arousal, and strong physical sensations. Bodily injury or violation may also be involved. Remembering trauma involves a sensorimotor re-experiencing (until processed into autobiographical memory) (Mollon, 2002). Although talking therapy can be helpful, it is often not adequate to resolve traumatic experience. Psychoanalytic talk therapy can facilitate insight, but seems often to leave the underlying dysfunctional patterns unchanged.

One of the first effective psychological treatments for trauma was eye movement desensitisation and reprocessing (EMDR). This involves sensorimotor activity (such as eye movements, bilateral tapping on the body, or auditory bilateral stimulation). It also involves a mindful awareness of bodily sensations—as well as attention to crucial cognitions. Thus it addresses body, emotions, and cognitions. Although originally framed within a cognitive-behavioural paradigm (Shapiro, 2001), EMDR accelerates the emergence of relevant psychodynamic material and facilitates free-association (Mollon, 2005a). It is indeed highly congruent with the original Freudian method.

Different forms of bilateral stimulation are effective, including tapping on the body. Bilateral tapping may be more calming, and less evocative of distress than eye movements. Back in the late 1990s and subsequently, many EMDR practitioners began to experiment with tapping on acupressure points—particularly following the internet dissemination of the simple EP method called emotional freedom techniques.

Energy and information in the body

"Energies" in the body can be experienced. We can think of the stronger forms of "psychic energy" of emotions, such as aggression or sexual arousal, which can be directed outwards or discharged on a person's own body. There are different qualities and intensities of energy, some more subtle. Compare, for example, the experienced energies of love, of sex, of a beautiful church, of a rock concert, of a Nazi rally—and of the personal energies of people who are calming (more yin) and those who are arousing or agitating (more yang).

The term "subtle energy" was first proposed by Professor William Tiller of Stamford University (Tiller, 1993). It was rediscovered many times (Swanson, 2010) by many different people, under many different names—such as Freud's libido, Reich's "orgone energy", Chi, Ki, Prana, Life Force, Elan Vitale (and many other names). For Freud, libido was not a metaphor but a tangible energy—a point particularly apparent in his concept of the "actual neuroses" (Freud, 1894a), which he described as neurotic states that were a direct result of inadequate (or excessive) discharge of sexual energy, contrasting with the "neuropsychoses of defence". Reich wrote of orgone in very similar ways to Freud's libido—as an energetic quantity that can flow, be blocked or diverted, and can become toxic.

Energy psychologists (beginning with Dr Roger Callahan, who drew on the earlier work of Dr John Diamond) discovered that the body's subtle energy system also contains *information* (Callahan, 2001). Here is how it came about. In the 1960s, Detroit chiropractor George Goodheart became intrigued by the functioning of muscles, prompted by a puzzling muscle phenomenon presented by a client.

He studied factors that affected muscle tone, using "manual muscle testing", whereby a degree of pressure is exerted by the practitioner's hand against the client's resistance. This revealed associations between particular muscle groups and particular states of physical sickness. However, he also noticed that when a person thought of something emotionally negative or distressing, their muscle tone became weak, but strong when they thought of something emotionally positive. Similarly, speaking an untruth made the muscle tone weak and speaking truth registered as strong. The use of muscle testing formed the basis of Goodheart's evolving field, known as applied kinesiology (Walther, 2000). Goodheart also explored links between his observations and what was known of the meridian system of acupuncture/acupressure. His associate, psychiatrist Dr John Diamond, explored muscle testing in a greatly expanded way, testing people to a wide range of stimuli, including music, visual images, facial expressions, foods, chemicals, etc. Amongst his many books is *Your Body Doesn't Lie* (Diamond, 1979), outlining his findings from muscle testing. Diamond also explored the meridians, using muscle testing (1985). He noted links between particular meridians and particular emotions. Moreover, he found that if a meridian was out of balance, it could be restored by having the person make a particular affirmation related to that meridian. In these exciting developments in the 1970s and 80s, for the first time in recorded history, links were being made between thoughts, emotions, words, muscles, and the body's subtle energy system. Whilst Freud had described dreams as the "royal road" to the unconscious, Diamond noted that muscle testing provided a more direct route!

Clinical psychologist Dr Roger Callahan had been studying with Goodheart and Diamond and others within the applied kinesiology group. In 1979 he had a patient, Mary, who had a long-standing phobia of water. She would avoid rain, rivers, the ocean—would drink as little water as possible, and did not like washing. This fear had dominated her life as long as she could remember. Callahan—at that time a cognitive therapist, in the Albert Ellis tradition—tried a variety of approaches, including cognitive, behavioural, and hypnotherapy, with very limited results. Mary could tolerate sitting with her feet dangling in his swimming pool, but would feel very uncomfortable. The anxiety would not settle. Callahan discerned, through muscle testing, that Mary's stomach meridian was registering an imbalance. Acting on a whim (as he described it), he asked her to tap under her eye (the start of the stomach meridian). After a few seconds, Mary exclaimed joyfully, "It's gone!"—and ran to the swimming pool to splash about. She subsequently explained that the anxiety she had constantly experienced in her stomach, whenever she thought of water, had instantly gone. Her fear never returned.

Astonished by this effect—one which he had never heard of before—Callahan tried asking his other patients to tap in a similar way. Results were discouraging. Fortunately, Callahan persisted, realising that he had stumbled across an important phenomenon. He found, by trial and exploration, a muscle testing procedure that provided sequences of meridians that needed to be tapped. Most of his patients needed to tap a sequence specific to them and their troubled state. By gradually refining his method, eliminating any unnecessary steps, Callahan developed a highly efficient procedure that relieved emotional distress in most cases. In published work (e.g., Callahan, 2001), he presented a series of "algorithms", the commonly occurring sequences of meridian tapping required for different emotional states. However, the muscle testing procedure for what he called "causal diagnosis" (which requires considerable practice to learn and become proficient in) remained the key to more focused and individual work.

Callahan called his method Thought Field Therapy, because his explorations revealed that the troubling *thought* (or memory) was expressed as *information* in the energy *field* of the body. A remarkable feature of Callahan's discoveries was that the thought can literally be seen, felt, and palpated through the muscle signalling system. The variations in muscle tone can be felt by the practitioner and client, and can be seen easily by observers. One demonstration I favour, in a lecture or workshop context, is to ask a volunteer to think of some troubling issue that he or she would like to feel better about. Callahan's muscle testing procedure (taught in his workshops) is then used to find the underlying meridian (and chakra) sequence, and to clear the emotional charge through tapping on this sequence of energy points. The distress collapses—even though the practitioner-demonstrator has no idea of the content of the troubling issue. In normal clinical practice, of course, there would be discussion of the content of the problem, but the demonstration reveals how the emotional perturbations (Callahan's preferred term) are expressed as specific informational codes in the body's energy field—and these codes can be seen and felt. The energetic information, *of the embodied thought*, is revealed and read via the muscle signalling system.

The emotional information in the meridian and chakra system is revealed to be digitally encoded as a sequence of on/off meridians. It appears to be the *emotion* that is encoded as this digital information, rather than the cognitive aspects of the thought field. Different meridians seem to express different emotions (as originally discovered by John Diamond), and so the meridian (and chakra) sequence may express the layering of emotions linked to an issue. The skilled practitioner may find that the emerging sequence of meridians (revealed through the muscle signalling) gives useful clues to the emotions that are about to become conscious at any particular moment. After successful "treatment" of a thought field, the thought or memory remains, but its distressing emotional charge is gone.

Whilst muscle testing, developed from Goodheart's field of applied kinesiology (Walther, 2000) and refined by Diamond (1985), provided the basis for all of energy psychology, it is not an essential feature of the work in its modern forms. Many modalities, such as the popular emotional freedom techniques (EFT)—which is a simplification of thought field therapy—do not use muscle testing at all. One interesting feature, commonly recognised by those who do use muscle testing, is that it can be done "by proxy" or "remotely". The practitioner can "self-test" in order to read the client's field. This enables telephone work, by suitably skilled practitioners. There are many intriguing "transpersonal" aspects of interpersonal reality revealed by muscle testing (whereby the informational energy field of one person connects with that of another), and such observations are commonplace in the energy psychology community.

In order to carry out this procedure in the clinic setting, therapist and client can sit in a position where repeated muscle testing is comfortable—side by side, or at an angle, rather than face to face. The physical touch consists of light pressure with the finger tips on the wrist. One workshop participant commented, "you seem to be listening with your fingertips"—and this phrase does seem to capture the subtle sensing that is required. This clinical touch does not appear to attract erotic meanings. It becomes part of the frame of therapy from the beginning.

Obstacles to healing

Two kinds of problems have been found to block the process of healing completely (until corrected). First, there can be systemic energy disturbances, such as "polarity reversal" (also known as "neurological disorganisation"), and "homolateral energy flow". These conditions have no psychological content, but simply reflect dysfunctional or suboptimal features of the energy system at that moment. Fortunately, these can usually be corrected simply and rapidly by certain energy procedures. The second kind of problem, called psychological reversal, was discovered by Dr Callahan. He found that some people who would not respond to his tapping procedures showed a revealing muscle test response. When asked to say "I want to be over this problem", their muscle would test weak, and when asked to say "I want to keep this problem" the muscle would test strong. Their system was "reversed" against recovery. Callahan noted a number of different variants of psychological reversal. Initially he did not know how to correct this. By trial and error, he found three simple procedures that would often help: (1) tapping the side of the hand on small intestine 2 acupoint; (2) making a statement of self-acceptance; (3) use of the Bach "rescue remedy". The most commonly used correction for psychological reversal is, in fact, the side of hand tap, often combined with a statement of self-acceptance (although Dr Callahan has now discarded the self-acceptance statement as unnecessary). Whilst psychological reversal can indeed be eliminated in this simple way, thereby allowing the rest of the tapping procedure to continue successfully, I find that the reversal can itself usefully be taken as a target, often then revealing and processing crucial childhood experiences to do with the origins of anxiety and injuries to self-esteem. Dr Callahan seemed not to emphasise the motivations behind reversals, but others (e.g., Gallo, 1999; Mollon, 2008) have done so. Common motives blocking resolution of a problem are: (1) it is not safe to do so; (2) the person feels he or she does not deserve to; (3) it would violate identity to do so; (4) the person is too angry and wishes to continue expressing suffering through the symptoms. Psychological reversal can thus also be framed as the "internal objections to change", and express the psychodynamics of the mind.

Is it a placebo effect?

A common response on hearing of the positive results of the energy psychology methods is that this obviously must be some kind of "placebo effect". Certainly, it is the case that placebo has an effect in many areas of medicine, including psychiatry. Brown (2013) notes that "For disorders in which psychotherapy works well, such as the less severe forms of depression and conditions characterised by anxiety, placebos also work well" (p. 100) and raises the possibility that "when all is said and done, psychotherapy's main benefit turns out to rest on maximising the placebo response" (p. 111). However, methods such as TFT are far from initially plausible to most clients, and seem unlikely to evoke easy belief in their likely effectiveness. Callahan (1985) comments:

> Another indication that this treatment is neither based on suggestion nor hypnosis is that I have successfully treated a number of people who not only did not have an open mind regarding what was taking place—they obviously were convinced I was some kind of madman. (p. 34)

It is actually the obstacles to healing, in the form of the systemic energy dysfunctions and the psychological reversals that are the most persuasive indicator that the therapeutic effects are real results of the procedure and not a more generalised placebo effect. This is because when these obstacles are present, they more or less completely block the therapeutic process. When they are identified and resolved—usually in a matter of a minute or so—the process that was blocked will now proceed easily. Most practitioners seem to find that when the therapeutic process is not evolving easily, there is always some energetic obstacle that can be located and addressed, then enabling the resolution of the target problem. However, it can take skill and sometimes persistent exploration to detect these obstacles.

Different levels of the mind–body energy system

Subtle energy, the medium of the information carrying morphogenetic field, appears to carry the blueprint for the more gross emotional energies expressed via the physiology. Resolving an emotional problem seems to be easiest if the work is done at a level above that at which the problem is manifest. Thus, resolving a problem of thoughts and feelings, by talking about thoughts and feelings, is hard and slow work—the traditional realm of psychotherapy. However, working from a level above—the energy body—is much faster and easier.

We may postulate that different therapies address different levels:

1. The physical body
2. The emotional body
3. The mental body
4. The energy body (and higher energy bodies).

Each level influences the one below and the one above. Effective work addresses the level above where the problem is manifest. For example, an effective therapy, such as EMDR, addresses the lower three levels, whereas less effective therapies may address only levels two or three. Energy psychology addresses level four as well. It is entirely feasible that even more effective methods will be developed that address higher levels still.

The sustained research project of William Tiller, Emeritus Professor of Materials Science at Stanford University is of relevance. In his book *Psychoenergetic Science: A Second Copernican-Scale Revolution* (2007), he describes his team's experimental work revealing the existence of "two unique levels of physical reality":

> These are: (1) Our conventional, particulate, electrical, atom/molecular level and (2) a new, magnetic, information wave level that has much in common with the old 'ether' concept of the 1800's. There also is **required** to exist a coupling medium, of a still higher dimensional nature, that allows these two, unique levels of physical reality to meaningfully interact. (p. xv)
> and
> This Level (2) aspect of physical reality responds to a very different type of physics. This latter aspect is modulateable by human consciousness, intention, emotion, mind and spirit! (p. xvi)

Tiller refers to an unstated assumption of physics that:

> No human qualities of consciousness, intention, emotion, mind or spirit can significantly influence a well-designed target experiment in physical reality. (p. 2)

His experiments have demonstrated this is quite wrong.

He has used an "Intention Imprinted Electrical Device" (IIED), which is a simple electrical circuit into which meditators, in an altered brain state, project a particular intention (possibly not dissimilar to some of the uses of a "radionics machine"). Such a device, imprinted with intention, has been shown to: (1) increase pH of water; (2) decrease pH of water; (3) increase activity of liver enzyme ALP in a solution; (4) to increase energy storage molecule ATP in fruit fly larvae—all at a distance.

Tiller concludes:

> We have discovered a second, unique level of physical reality that is quite different from our normal electric atom/molecule level ... The 'stuff' of this physical vacuum level consists of magnetic information waves ... We have observed that the physics of this new level is modulatable by the human mind, human intentions and human consciousness in general. (p. 13)

Most crucially for energy psychology, Tiller finds that the *human subtle energy system* is the portal, or "coupler system" to this level two reality that is at a higher dimensional level than level one physical reality. He poses the question:

> Is it possible that when a human being is born, there exists an organ or body system that is at the higher electromagnetic symmetry state (higher thermodynamic free energy per unit volume state)? If so, then this could drive all the processes (mechanical, chemical, electrical and optical) of the rest of the body and would look like a *source* of life. (p. 88)

His experiments demonstrate that "our acupuncture meridian/chakra system is the human body system that is at this higher thermodynamic free energy per unit volume state" (p. 89). Tiller revises Einstein's principle of "mass—energy" to "mass—energy—information—consciousness".

Tiller's experiments reveal the normal laws of physics and behaviour of the physical world alter in the presence of subtle energy. One example is the apparent occurrence of "magnetic monopoles"—a theoretical possibility that is not thought normally to exist—one side of a magnet increased enzyme effects (when within a room conditioned with subtle energy), whilst the other side of the magnet decreased the enzyme activity. These effects did not occur in a normal environment not conditioned with subtle energy. The human energy system also responds differently to different sides of a magnet (easily demonstrable). These phenomena do not make sense in terms of conventional physics.

Attachment and transpersonal aspects

The human energy system can read the energy field of another living entity. A simple demonstration of this is to muscle test a person as they look at an item of organic food and a similar looking item of non-organic food (without their conscious knowledge of which is which). The organic item (in my experience) always tests strong and the non-organic tests weak—to a degree that is disconcerting to witness.

Moreover, it seems that human beings are continuously intercommunicating energy fields, registering our living and physical environment. Thus, projection, projective identification, transference and countertransference are seen to have a tangible energetic reality. Telepathy can be revealed as a normal human phenomenon. It seems that client and therapist form one communicative energy field. Relevant thoughts, images, emotions, may occur anywhere in that shared "thought field"—in the client's mind or speech, in the therapist's mind or speech, or somewhere in the discourse between them.

These observations have some implications for our understanding of our early attachment history and the emotional information transmitted down the generational lines. We are conceived and grow within the mother's energy field, as well as carrying a fractal energy field of the father in the original sperm cell. Muscle testing data suggests that we are imprinted with the information in the parental energy fields, and their ancestral lines—but particularly the energy field of the mother. Perhaps we continue to be affected by our mother's energy field (regardless of distance). Adults seem more affected by encounters with their mothers than with their fathers.

A mother or other primary caregiver who is depressed, with a reversed energy field, is experienced, by energetic resonance, as disapproving and life-denying. Severe depression is a complete reversal of life energy, such that the system becomes death- seeking. This can have a negative (entraining) effect on those in close communication, such as children, other relatives, or the therapist. It is a transpersonal effect. Hyperactivity in children can sometimes appear to be an attempt to escape the depressed and reversed energy field of the mother—a manic flight followed by being "pulled back"—laying the basis for bipolar phenomena.

The integrity and autonomy of the energy field is an important consideration. Sometimes there are breaches or "holes" in the body's energy field, the auric "skin", which can allow leakage of life energy or intrusions of parasitic energy fields. The phenomenon of energy field entrainment is also of note—illustrated in crowd behaviour, demagogue phenomena, hypnotism, and spiritual healing. A state of health appears to be one that maintains its integrity, being relatively immune to intrusive influence.

Psychoanalytic energy psychotherapy (PEP)

There are many modalities of energy psychology. My own approach (Mollon, 2008), derived from my background as a psychoanalyst, is described as psychoanalytic energy psychotherapy (PEP). Whilst having much in common with other energy psychology methods, some of the more distinct features of this are as follows:

- Allowing the meridians and chakras to "speak", by frequently prompting, "Speak of whatever comes to mind", whilst the client is tapping.
- Reading the client's energy field to enable a continuously evolving dynamic process, in which there is a concurrent flow of energy, thought, and emotion.
- Taking particular note of the motivations behind the psychological reversals—and often choosing to track the roots and origins of these (by finding the evolving meridian sequence underpinning this phrase, and prompting the client to speak of what comes to mind).
- Careful use of words and phrases—succinct dynamic statements—to activate and tune the thought field.
- Checking for hidden areas of distress in the unconscious mind, dissociated parts, and the body.
- A stance of viewing the work as exploration of the unknown—an energetic as well as psychodynamic inquiry (rather than taking the presenting problem as the immediate target).

Transference and EP

Psychotherapists are often intrigued by energy psychology, but feel at a loss as to how such seemingly "different" methods might be integrated into more conventional work. In particular, psychotherapists often worry about the impact of adjunctive methods upon the therapeutic frame and the transference. Such issues become less of a problem if energy psychology methods are part of the frame from the beginning. Transference does emerge—briefly—but is more akin to Freud's original view of transference as an intrusive memory temporarily experienced as real in the present. This original (and important) perspective has been largely lost in much contemporary psychoanalytic work (Mollon, 2005b, 2011). It is worth reminding ourselves of what Freud, the originator of the concept of transference, actually said about it. In his 1895 *Studies in Hysteria*, he wrote: "Transference onto the physician takes place through a false connection", which he states "is a frequent, and in some analyses a regular, occurrence" (p. 302).

The idea of a "false connection" clearly implies something that is in need of correction—and certainly not a phenomenon to be encouraged. In his "Beyond the Pleasure Principle" (1920), he wrote:

> He (the patient) is obliged to *repeat* the repressed material as a contemporary experience instead of, as the physician would prefer to see, *remembering* it as something belonging to the past.
>
> It has been the physician's endeavour to keep this transference neurosis within the narrowest limits: to force as much as possible into the channel of memory and to allow as little as possible to emerge as repetition. (1920, pp. 18–19)

Frequently, psychoanalytic therapists are startled by an encounter with Freud's statement that the task is to "force as much as possible into the channel of memory and to allow as little as possible to emerge as repetition". It is so at odds with the prevailing fashion of focusing exclusively on the here-and-now relationship and "working through in the transference" as the vehicle of healing. Some might think the view expressed here was just an early position that Freud subsequently revised. This hypothesis is dispelled by consideration of the following passage from Freud's final book, *An Outline of Psychoanalysis* (1940):

> The danger of these states of transference evidently lies in the patient's misunderstanding their nature and taking them for fresh real experiences instead of reflections of the past ... It is the analyst's task constantly to tear the patient out of his *menacing illusion* and to show him again and again that what he takes to be new real life is a reflection of the past. (1940, pp. 176–177, italics added)

Energy psychology methods seem very suited to shifting brief intrusions of transference rapidly back into the realm of memory, where they belong. Instead of the theatre of the transference and the therapeutic relationship being the main vehicles of healing (as in conventional psychotherapy), the work in energy psychotherapy becomes much more focused within the client's system—not just intra-psychically, but intra-energetically, even though the therapeutic relationship, including its transpersonal aspects, may facilitate this.

Brief clinical example using psychoanalytic energy psychotherapy

Jenny, a professional woman in her mid-thirties, sought help for problems of anger and also headaches, which she suspected might be related. Often she would find herself feeling more angry than circumstances would seem to justify. Previously she had tried various therapies, including CBT and psychodynamic counselling, all of which had helped only slightly.

During our first meeting, Jenny talked for half an hour or so about various aspects of her life, including her marriage, her job, and her childhood. We then moved into some energy work, including muscle testing to bring the body into the therapeutic conversation. The initial step was some simple checks on her systemic energy state, having Jenny place her hand palm down over her head and then palm up, whilst I pressed lightly on her outstretched arm. This check revealed that her system lacked clear polarity at that point—showing no discernable difference in muscle tone with these two positions. I asked her to drink a glass of water (a commonly required correction). Following this, her system showed the correct polarisation (strong to palm down and weak to palm up)—and thus her energy was now flowing more freely and generating clear signals. This kind of common "systemic energy interference" has no psychological significance, but it does prevent easy energy work until corrected (e.g., by drinking a glass of water).

Next I muscle tested Jenny whilst she made a statement designed to reveal a generalised "psychological reversal" if one were present. I pressed lightly on her wrist a moment after she uttered the words, "I want to be well". Her muscle tone actually went weak to this. When I tested her to the statement, "I want to be sick", her arm was strong—indicating that at that moment her system was oriented towards illness and opposed to recovery. Often this kind of psychological reversal will respond to tapping a point on the small intestine meridian on the side of the hand. In this case it did not. I was puzzled. A generalised reversal of this kind is not particularly common, except amongst people who are very depressed or very ill. I asked her what came to mind. She could not think of anything initially, but as she continued tapping the side of the hand she suddenly remarked, "I think it is that when I was a child the only time I really got my mother's attention was when I was physically ill—the rest of the time I had to be looking after her—she was always tired and depressed!". I then asked her to continue tapping the side of the hand whilst saying, "Even though I want to be sick, because that was the only time I got my mother's attention, I completely accept myself". Following this, her arm tested strong to the statement, "I want to be well". It was important to work initially on this general reversal because energy psychologists have found that reversals will completely block resolution of a problem—so that we could have "tapped until the cows come home" without success. Fortunately, correction of reversals, even when somewhat tenacious, as in this case, normally takes only a few minutes at most.

It was not clear from Jenny's discourse up to this point what issue would be best to take as an initial focus. Therefore, I muscle tested Jenny as she uttered the phrase "the priority issue", on the assumption that her system would know what was the priority even if neither of us did so consciously—this reliance on the wisdom of the unconscious of the "system as a whole" is a common feature of energy psychological work, well grounded in clinicians' experience of the reliability of this trust. As expected, Jenny's arm went weak to this phrase (because her system would be accessing an area of distress). We scanned the meridians (a process too complex to describe here) and when we focused on the central vessel (when Jenny touched a point on her chin), her arm locked strong. I asked her to tap on this point and to speak of whatever came to mind. This energy pathway is associated with shame, although Jenny was not aware of this. She began to speak of a memory that had just come to her mind of a humiliating experience in hospital aged five. She had been admitted with abdominal pains—and had been told off by a nurse for wetting the bed. The next energy point to register in the emerging sequence was her throat chakra—often associated with unexpressed feelings and thoughts. As she tapped her fingers in the field of the throat chakra she began to think of how she had withdrawn in her shame in this scene in the hospital—and how this withdrawal and silencing of her feelings had been a general part of her childhood pattern, at home as well as in that specific hospital situation. The next energy point to emerge was her gall bladder meridian. As Jenny tapped the side of the eye, she began to feel much more aware of the underlying rage she had felt towards the nurse who shamed her. Continuing to tap on this point, she began to see how suppression of her rage had been a chronic feature of her relationship with her rather controlling mother. She began to speak of how her mother had always seemed very preoccupied with good behaviour and appearances, responding with cold withdrawal and criticism to any of Jenny's behaviour or emotions that she deemed insufficiently polite and graceful. The next energy point to emerge was the stomach meridian, often associated with anxiety—as Jenny began to appreciate how frightened she had felt of her mother's disapproval and shaming.

Up to this point, the emphasis had been upon "allowing the meridians and chakras to speak". We were exploring the meridian and chakra coding underpinning the phrase "the priority issue". By asking Jenny to speak of whatever came to mind whilst she tapped on the emerging sequence of meridians and chakras, we allowed the emotional and cognitive material associated with each point to be expressed. Now that we were getting an indication of the significance of repeated experiences of her mother's disapproval and shaming, I shifted tack slightly by using the phrase "all the times and ways my mother criticised and shamed me, and all its effects on me"—again following the underlying meridian and chakra sequence, as revealed by muscle testing. As Jenny continued tapping, she displayed brief moments of strong emotion—including fear, shame, and rage—before becoming calm. We continued for several minutes until her arm remained strong to the phrase we were using. The strong arm would indicate that distress, or "perturbations" (as Callahan would call them), were no longer associated with this phrase—and this did indeed coincide with Jenny's subjective experience of feeling very calm.

This session lasted about an hour and a half. We agreed that Jenny would monitor her states of mind and behaviour over the next week or so, and she could contact me again for further work if she felt it necessary. I recommended she be open to whatever reactions she might observe—and that she might continue feeling calm, or she might find that other emotional material surfaces into the space that had been cleared in her system. Subsequently, Jenny did report a lessening in her propensity for anger and headaches. However, she did request further work relating to issues in her marriage, which turned out to be closely linked to experiences with her father, whom she felt had been insufficiently supportive in her struggles with her mother.

Core principles and procedures of EP

It is possible to state the principles and procedures common to the different energy psychology approaches broadly as follows. The therapist and client together will:

1. Activate the subtle energy system
2. Use intention combined with physical stimulation of the energy system
3. Target first the internal objections to change (psychological reversal)
4. Then target the "thought field" of distress.

In order to do the work of energy psychotherapy adequately, all the skills of conventional psychotherapy are required—including an understanding of personality development, attachment, psychodynamics of conflict, transference and countertransference, and role of trauma. In addition the following skills and knowledge are required:

- Awareness of the subtle energy systems, including meridians and chakras—and how to work with these therapeutically
- A capacity to "read" the client's energy field
- Sensitivity to the movement of subtle energy.

Fortunately ... All these are teachable!

Some conclusions

Energy psychology can be welcomed as a potent addition to our therapeutic perspectives and methods, enabling creative access to a realm of the human system that hitherto was obscured. Since the patterns of psychological and somatic dysfunction appear to be patterned in this higher dimensional realm, resolution of these is easier when we work at this level of the system. This higher dimensional realm is, paradoxically, also a very bodily realm. By drawing upon it, we bring more levels of the person into the psychotherapeutic conversation. Energy psychology does not make other psychotherapeutic skills redundant, nor is it a panacea for all of human suffering. Moreover, our current theorising, including the speculations articulated in this paper, may turn out to be mistaken. What seems clear, however, is that EP methods work—they bring relief rapidly and with less distress than many other approaches.

References

Brown, W. A. (2013). *The Placebo Effect in Clinical Practice*. New York: Oxford University Press.

Callahan, R. J. (1981). Psychological reversal. Paper presented at the proceedings of the International College of Applied Kinesiology, Winter Meeting, Acapulco, Mexico.

Callahan, R. J. (1985). *How Executives Overcame the Fear of Public Speaking and Other Phobias*. Wilmington, DE: Enterprise Publishing.

Callahan, R. J. (2001). *Tapping the Healer Within*. Chicago: Contemporary Books.

Church, D., Hawk, C., Brooks, A., Toukolehto, O., Wren, M., Dinter, I., & Stein, P. (2013). Psychological trauma symptom improvement in veterans using emotional freedom techniques: a randomized controlled trial. *Journal of Nervous and Mental Diseases, 201*(2): 153–160.

Church, D., Piña, O., Reategui, C., & Brooks, A. (2012). Single session reduction of the intensity of traumatic memories in abused adolescents after EFT: A randomized controlled pilot study. *Traumatology, 18*(3): 73–79. doi:10.1177/1534765611426788.

Church, D., Yount, G., & Brooks, A. (2012). The effect of emotional freedom technique (EFT) on stress biochemistry: A randomized controlled trial. *Journal of Nervous and Mental Diseases, 200*(10): 891–896. doi: 10.1097/NMD.0b013e31826b9fc1.

Connolly, S., & Sakai, C. (2011). Brief trauma intervention with Rwandan genocide survivors using thought field therapy. *International Journal of Emergency Mental Health, 13*(3): 161–172.
Diamond, J. (1979). *Your Body Doesn't Lie*. New York: Harper and Row.
Diamond, J. (1985). *Life Energy*. New York: Dodd, Mead & Co.
Diamond, J. (1988). *Life Energy Analysis. A Way to Cantillation*. New York: Archaeus.
Fang, J., Jin, Z., Wang, Y., Li, K., Kong, J., Nixon, E. E., Zeng, Y., Ren, Y., Tong, H., Wang, Y., Wang, P., & Hui, K. K. (2009). The salient characteristics of the central effects of acupuncture needling: Limbic-paralimbic-neocortical network modulation. *Human Brain Mapping, 30*: 1196–1206.
Feinstein, D. (2012). Acupoint stimulation in treating psychological disorders. Evidence of efficacy. *Review of General Psychology, 16*(4): 364–380.
Freud, S. (1894a). The neuropsychoses of defence. *S. E., 3*. London: Hogarth.
Freud, S. (1920g). Beyond the pleasure principle. *S. E., 18*: 1–64. London: Hogarth.
Freud, S. (1923b). The ego and the id. *S. E., 19*: 1–66. London: Hogarth.
Freud, S., & Breuer, J. (1895d) *Studies on hysteria. S. E., 2*. London: Hogarth.
Gallo, F. P. (1999). *Energy Psychology*. Boca Raton, FL: CRC Press.
Karatzias, T., Power, K., Brown, K., McGoldrick, T., Begum, M., Young, J., & Adams, S. (2011). A controlled comparison of the effectiveness and efficiency of two psychological therapies for posttraumatic stress disorder: eye movement desensitization and reprocessing vs. emotional freedom techniques. *Journal of Nervous & Mental Disease, 199*, 372–378.
Mollon, P. (2002). *Remembering Trauma. A Psychotherapist's Guide to Memory and Illusion* (2nd edn). London: Whurr.
Mollon, P. (2005a). *EMDR and the Energy Therapies. Psychoanalytic Perspectives*. Karnac: London.
Mollon, P. (2005b). The abandonment of memory, trauma, and sexuality: the excessive preoccupation with 'transference', and other problems with contemporary psychoanalysis. In: P. Mollon, *EMDR and the Energy Therapies, Psychoanalytic Perspectives* (pp. 71–95). Karnac: London.
Mollon, P. (2008). *Psychoanalytic Energy Psychotherapy*. Karnac: London.
Mollon, P. (2011). The foreclosure of the Freudian transference in modern British technique. *Psychoanalytic Inquiry, 31*(1): 28–41.
Reich, W. R. (1942). *The Function of the Orgasm. Sex-economic Problems of Biological Energy*. New York: Orgone Institute Press.
Shapiro, F. (2001). *Eye Movement Desensitisation and Reprocessing* (2nd edn). New York: Guilford Press.

Strachey, J. (1962). The emergence of Freud's fundamental hypotheses. In: S. Freud, *S. E.*, *3*: 62–68. London: Hogarth.
Tiller, W. A. (1993). What are subtle energies? *Journal of Scientific Exploration*, 7(3): 293–304.
Tiller, W. A. (2007). *Psychoenergetic Science. A Second Copernican-Scale Revolution*. Walnut Creek, CA: Pavior.
Walther, D. S. (2000). *Applied Kinesiology: Synopsis* (2nd edn). Shawnee Mission, KS: Triad of Health Publishing.

CHAPTER FIVE

Wisdom of the body, lost and found: the nineteenth John Bowlby Memorial Lecture

Pat Ogden

Our physical actions are guided by predictions of the immediate future. Every waking moment we are exposed to an enormous amount of sensory stimulation from the immediate environment, as well as to the variety of our own internal emotions, thoughts, body sensations, images, and movements. In milliseconds our brains must perform amazingly complex operations to compare this data to our past experience. The chief purpose of these computations is to anticipate the potential outcomes of various actions and choose an action that is expected to have the best possible outcome in terms of survival (Llinas, 2001). Roger Sperry stated in 1952 that the brain is "first and foremost an organ of movement" (Van der Kolk, 2006, p. xviii). But before we move our bodies, we must predict the immediate future; in fact, Siegel (1999) describes the brain as an "anticipation machine." Every single move we make from reaching out for help to reaching for a glass of water is the result of our anticipation of what will occur in the very next moment.

Many of our predictions, especially those that pertain to interactions with others, have taken shape prior to the acquisition of language. Beebe (2006) asserts:

> Predictability and expectancy is a key organizing principle of the infant's brain. Infants form expectancies of how ... interactions go, whether they are positive or negative, and these expectancies set a trajectory for development (which can nevertheless transform). (p. 160)

These implicit predictions influence not only the developing brain, but also the body and its movements. A powerful indication of the wisdom of the body is that its movement, posture, and physiology will adapt without conscious intent in order to assure survival and maximise available resources. This chapter will explore this innate wisdom of the body, elucidate how the body and brain adjust to environmental conditions and relational dynamics, and illustrate how physical action can become a viable target for psychotherapeutic intervention.

Implicit relational knowing and working models

"Implicit relational knowing," defined as "how to do things with others" (Lyons-Ruth, 1998) has its beginnings in infant interactions with attachment figures. These early relationships strongly influence the child's developing cognition, affect array, regulatory ability, and movement patterns: the way the child holds his or her body, and executes particular gestures and facial expressions, and so forth. This knowing, shaped by memories that are unavailable to conscious recollection and organised on a primitive and fundamental level (Piaget, 1962), is devoid of conscious understanding and verbal description, but yet potently predicts what vocalisations, expressions and actions will be welcomed or rejected by others.

Over time, infants will learn to repeat the expressions, postures, movements and gestures that elicit a desired response from their attachment figures, or, at least in traumatogenic environments, minimise abuse and neglect. The repeated execution of a particular movement will influence the shape of the body. For example, a typical movement made in response to being afraid is to hunch the shoulders. If a child lives in an atmosphere of fear, this movement may be executed over and over, and can become a habitual way of holding the shoulders. Called "procedural learning," such habits are reliable and enduring once they are learned. A procedural skill, such as riding a bike or tying a shoelace, endures over time and is easily executed even years after the last time a bike was ridden or a shoelace was tied. Similarly, ways of holding the body and executing actions learned in the context of attachment relationships (such as hunching the shoulders) persist long after the circumstances that elicited these actions are over. Once learned, procedural actions do not "require conscious or unconscious mental representations, images, motivations or ideas to operate" (Grigsby & Stevens, 2000, p. 316) but involve automatic, reflexive performance of the movement. Because the memories that shape procedural learning commence in infancy (Tulving & Schacter, 1990), they are typically unavailable to verbal recall, reflection and evaluation.

Procedural learning reflects internal working models. These models "are based on that person's forecasts of how accessible and responsive his attachment figures are likely to be should he turn to them for support." (Bowlby, 1973, p. 203). They hone our implicit relational knowing by helping us perceive situations, predict the future, and construct plans of action (Bowlby, 1973). Encoded in procedural memory, our working models constrain the meaning we make of each moment, and become non-conscious strategies of affect regulation (Schore, 1994) and relational interaction. Meaning-making is usually thought of as a conscious and verbal process, but a wide variety of human capacities and phenomena influence and express meanings. Tronick (2009) confirms:

> Meanings include anything from the linguistic, symbolic, abstract realms, which we easily think of as forms of meaning, to the bodily, physiologic, behavioural and emotional structures and processes, which we find more difficult to conceptualise as forms, acts, or actualizations of meaning. (p. 88)

The symbols and language that express conscious meanings are perhaps less critical for psychotherapy practice than the variety of automatic implicit patterns (such as gesture, posture, prosody, facial expressions, eye gaze, and movement habits) that both reflect and sustain unconscious working models.

Working models and their physical actions help children to cope with trauma and inadequate attachment, as well as maximise the resources of the environment and the people in it. For example, if attachment figures expect their daughter to be obedient and unassertive, she might slump and keep her body small in order to gain their approval. On the other hand, if attachment figures expect her to be strong and assertive, she might unconsciously lift her chin and puff up her chest so that they accept her. Children adjust their inner needs to parental demands and preferences, learning early on what is expected in relationships, and their bodies both reflect and sustain these expectations. Perhaps a client has abandoned standing proudly upright with a straightforward gaze into the eyes of another, for a collapsed posture and averted gaze that prevents intimate engagement with others, or prevents his being seen fully by them, or both.

Trauma stimulates another kind of somatic intelligence in the form of instinctive defensive responses designed to assure survival. Under threat, the sympathetic nervous systems release adrenalin to stimulate the heart to pump harder and to increase respiration, providing muscles with the oxygen and energy needed to fuel the animal defences of fight or escape. All the senses become hyper alert. But often, fighting back or running away is impossible, or would only make the trauma worse, as is the case in childhood trauma. The next line of defence is to protect by becoming numb, frozen, collapsed, and immobilised. These innate physical and physiological responses to trauma are essential to our survival.

What were initially adaptive responses to danger and to surviving attachment relationships often continue long after conditions have changed. Decades afterwards, clients may still experience physical reactions that they experienced during the initial situations. Those who suffered trauma may continue to feel frozen, numb, or tense, or be constantly ready to fight or flee. They may be hyper alert, overly sensitive to sounds or movements, and easily startled by unfamiliar stimuli. Or they may underreact to stimuli, feel distant from their experience and their bodies, and even have a sense of deadness. Our clients also embody the postural and movement habits that helped to maximise the resources that their attachment figures could offer them. But often neither clients nor their therapists understand the original wisdom of these physical reactions and do not realise that addressing them in therapy can provide avenues to help them move beyond the confines of the past.

Self-states and the complexity of working models

Working models that fuel forecasts of the future can be complex and may even be even contradictory. Bowlby (1982) asserts, "… it is not uncommon for an individual to operate, simultaneously, with two (or more) working models of his attachment figure(s) and two (or more) working models of himself" (p. 205). When multiple models of a single figure are operative, they are likely to differ in regard to their origin, their dominance, and the extent to which the subject is aware of them (p. 205).

Different working models may be held by different self-states, and also have differing forecasts of the future. Bromberg (2011) clarifies how these different self-states come about:

> A person's core self—the self that is shaped by early attachment patterns—is defined by who the parental objects both perceive him to be and deny him to be. That is, through relating to their child as though he is "such and such" and ignoring other aspects of him as if they don't exist, the parents "disconfirm" the relational existence of those aspects of the child's self that they perceptually dissociate .... The main point is that "disconfirmation" ... is relationally nonnegotiable ... (p. 57)

Many clients seem to find it impossible to reconcile various self-states and their contradictory working models formed in relationship to attachment figures, such as a needy young self with a confident, independent adult self. Simon, a young college student in his early twenties, felt that ever since he could remember, he had "always been independent and a loner." Growing up in a traumatogenic environment, he said that there was never anyone to turn to, so he had never relied on anyone for help, advice, or comfort. We can surmise that his attachment figures denied his own dependency and need for attachment as a child in favour of confirming an independent, competent attitude. His "needy self" had become a "not-me" self-state that he disdained.

Traumatised clients often experience a vacillation between intrusive reliving of past trauma and numb avoidance of traumatic reminders. The reliving phase is accompanied by dysregulated autonomic arousal and animal defences, and the avoidance phase is accompanied by constriction, loss of energy, and diminished pleasure (Chu, 1998; Van der Hart, Nijenhuis & Steele, 2006; Van der Kolk, McFarlane & Weisaeth, 1996). Traumatic reminders repeatedly ignite subcortical survival responses—animal defences of fight, flight, freeze, and feigned death, interrupting activities of daily life as the individual prepares to defend against stimuli assessed as threatening. But it is also necessary to refocus on non-threatening activities—relationships and work—which require that stimuli associated with the trauma are avoided. However, biphasic alternations between re-experiencing traumatic reminders (which elicits animal defence) and avoiding them in order to engage in daily life can result in the encoding of self-states. Each hold procedurally learned tendencies and working models associated with these two situations. These trauma-related self-states are prepared for threat, and become dissociative parts that are dysregulated, discontinuous, often disruptive to daily life, and resistant to integration. Simon had been abused throughout his childhood by both parents, and close relationships were a primary trigger for him. He found himself reacting defensively when people came near him, or touched him, to the point of reactive violence.

Each moment offers an opportunity to integrate disparate self-states, change their working models and their predictions. Llinas (2001) asserts that as we compare the present moment with the past, "an 'upgrading' [occurs] of the internal image of what is to come to its actualization into the external world" (p. 38). Yet, like the part of Simon that reacted so violently to closeness, particular self-states can continue to operate on working models that were adaptive in the past, and physical movements are both constrained and reinforced by their predictions. Trauma and attachment experience, with their consequential neuropsychological deficits, often prevent "upgrading the forecast" because brains are conservative in taking the risk that outcomes of certain actions might be "safe" when they were once "dangerous." The lack of upgrading, of course, serves survival functions (better to mistake a stick for a snake than a snake for a stick) but also can thwart adaptive action in favour of what has worked in past circumstances.

Each self-state has its own perspective of reality, which they do not communicate to one another explicitly. As Bromberg (2012) confirms, "The felt otherness between one's own states becomes an alien 'thing' to be managed because it can no longer be contained as negotiable internal conflict that is mediated by self–other wholeness" (p. 274). Simon had great difficulty holding the differing "truths" of his different self-states in mind at the same time. His way of managing this conflict was to deny the emotionally needy self-state, the "not-me" self state that he scorned. However, doing so squelched a voice inside him that needed to be heard, and would eventually show its face in desire for human contact.

Our clients' behaviour is alive in the present with action sequences that reveal the various self-states connected with painful histories, even in the context of a "safe" therapeutic alliance. Bromberg (2006) clarifies that

> the dissociated horror of the past fills the present with affective meaning so powerful that no matter how 'obviously' safe a given situation may be to others, a client's perceptual awareness that he himself is safe would require a moment of consciousness that could potentially increase self-reflective capacity and thereby decrease reliance on dissociative hypervigilance ... Relaxing one's dissociative hypervigilance entails a risk that is felt as too dangerous to the client's felt stability of selfhood. (p. 180)

Particular self-states can be threatened by that which would challenge the veracity of their working models. Simon's confident, smart self-state was definitely threatened by the "needy" part of him that held a completely different working model. The "horror of the past" can show itself in a variety of physical actions: the constriction or collapse of the body, the shaking of a dysregulated nervous system, tension in the larynx and tightness in the voice reflecting a loss of social engagement, or in the avoidance of or locking in of eye contact. It is clear from such non-verbal behaviours that the self-states of many clients, including Simon's, forecast the future as grim and filled with peril, no matter how strongly other self-states refute this position and describe the future as different from the past.

Indicators of self-states and working models

Visible and tangible non-verbal behaviours are viable targets of intervention in the therapy hour. Kurtz states that non-verbal "indicators" are "a piece of behaviour or an element of style or anything that suggests ... a connection to character, early memories, or particular [unconscious] emotions" especially those that reflect and sustain predictions that are "protective, over-generalized and outmoded" (2010, p. 110).

Indicators are that those non-verbal behaviours that help the therapist (implicitly and explicitly) begin to form hypotheses about the kinds of working models that are expressed by different self-states, their physical patterns, and what type of early attachment relationships might have called for such adaptations. Indicators that either client or therapist notice can be explored explicitly, even if the content they represent remains unconscious. Exploring the indicators naturally stimulates curiosity and facilitates awareness of actions, memories, and affects associated with them.

Therapist and client together interrupt the automaticity of these indicators when they become mindful of them, "not as disease or something to be rid of, but in an effort to help the client become conscious of how experience is managed and how the capacity for experience can be expanded" (Kurtz, 1990, p. 111). Note that the general notion of mindful attention as being receptive to whatever elements emerge in the mind's eye is different from mindful attention directed specifically toward non-verbal indicators. Instead of allowing clients' attention to drift randomly toward whatever emotions, memories, or thoughts or physical actions might emerge, therapists use "directed mindfulness" to guide the client's awareness toward particular indicators that provide a jumping-off point for exploration of self-states and working models (Ogden, 2007, 2009). It takes intention, experience and practice for the therapist to "know" which non-verbal cues are indicators and which are not. This "knowing" is not cognitive; rather the therapist finds him or herself being drawn to a specific non-verbal cue, often with not knowing why. Typically, later discoveries in the therapy hour reveal that the cue was a significant indicator of working models, defensive response, and attachment history that reflect and sustain self-states.

Using mindfulness in psychotherapy practice privileges awareness of the moment-by-moment *experience* of implicit patterns over formulating a cohesive narrative, engaging in conversation, or "talking about" (Kurtz, 1990; Ogden & Minton, 2000; Ogden, Minton & Pain, 2006). There are many definitions of mindfulness. Several psychotherapeutic methods have been developed that teach mindfulness through structured exercises, practices, and sets of skills. In Linehan's (1993) model, for example, clients are taught mindfulness "what" skills of observing, describing, and participating, as well as "how" skills of focusing on one thing at a time and being effective.

Building on Buddhist perspectives, Kurtz (2004) describes the essence of mindfulness:

to be fully present to our [internal] experience, what-ever it is: our thoughts, images, memories, breath, body sensations, the sounds and smells and tastes, moods and feelings and the quality of our whole experience as well as of the various parts. Mindfulness is not our notions about our experience, but even noticing the notions. (p. 39)

Influenced by Kurtz, sensorimotor psychotherapy uses a specific clinical "map" for the purpose of inquiring into the direct moment-by-moment internal experience of working models. In a therapy hour, the therapist attends both to following the client's narrative or "story", and tracking present-moment internal experience—emotions, thoughts, five-sense perception, movements, and body sensations—that emerge spontaneously. These five elements comprise the present-moment internal experience of every waking moment but often occur outside of awareness and become the focal points of mindful exploration and change in the therapy hour (cf. Ogden, Minton & Pain, 2006).

Instead of conversation, present moment experience becomes a target of mindful exploration. In particular, procedural actions can be inroads into their working models and the troubled early histories that shaped them. The automaticity of physical actions are interrupted by becoming mindful of them, and by doing so the client can identify, rather than identify with, working models and self-states (Ogden, Minton & Pain, 2006). Importantly, unlike most other mindfulness disciplines, in sensorimotor psychotherapy mindfulness is integrated with and embedded within what transpires moment-to-moment between therapist and client, rather than taught through structured exercises or practices (Ogden, in press).

Proximity-seeking actions, regulated by the attachment system, are powerful avenues of exploration in therapy. Infants and children need the proximity of a supportive other to meet their survival needs and protect them from danger. Bowlby (1982) states that the psychobiological attachment system organises proximity-seeking behaviours to secure the nearness of attachment figures in two primary ways: signalling behaviour, which is designed to bring the attachment figure closer, and approach behaviour, which is designed to bring the individual closer to the attachment figure. This innate system adjusts to the behaviour of the attachment figures. If the attachment figure is unreliable, the proximity-seeking behaviours may become hyperactive. If the attachment figure is neglectful or unavailable, or punishing in the face of need or vulnerability, the proximity-seeking behaviours may become hypoactive.

Proximity-seeking actions, such as eye contact, reaching out, or decreasing distance may be conflicted and emotionally painful actions for a client with a troubled attachment history, filled with meaning and working models. Children wisely stop reaching out if they expect no one to be there to reach back; they cease making eye contact if they expect to see disapproval or rejection in their parents' eyes. Often, as the client/therapist relationship develops, hints of proximity-seeking actions may emerge in sessions, but are truncated before they are fully executed because they were implicitly fraught with pain and fear of what might happen if proximity were achieved. Examples might be a slight opening of the hand, the beginning attempt to reach out: fleeting, inconsistent eye contact; or an almost imperceptible leaning forward toward the analyst, subtly decreasing the physical distance between them. Or clients may demonstrate proximity-distancing actions such as physically leaning away from the therapist, flat prosody devoid of affect, absence of eye contact, or habitual gestures that convey a "keep back" or "stay away" message, such as lifting of the fingers or hands, palms facing outward.

Clinical example

Simon's therapy illustrates select indicators and examples of how to use embedded relational mindfulness to work with proximity-seeking and distancing actions in clinical practice. At the first session, Simon expressed that his main goal in therapy was to "get over the shock response" to touch. He reported: "Basically it's like since going through a lot of very different emotionally damaging situations, I guess, when someone—I guess anybody—if they touch me, and if I perceive that they are judging me in any way, my immediate response is to tense up and push them away physically. Since I also have the background of originally being a fighter, I can always defend myself. But this leads to me getting into little petty fights. I also don't like being in large groups of people ... I get anxious." Simon stated that his aversion to touch began around the age of six, when physical and sexual abuse began; he doesn't remember anything before that time. Simon had great difficulty navigating proximity, and negotiating physical distance became a fruitful task in our therapy.

Simon and I decided to explore his responses to proximity by my leaning forward slightly to decrease the distance between us, mindfully enacting together a situation that triggers him: people being close to him. I asked Simon to notice his automatic responses as I leaned forward, and he reported that he tensed up. I remarked that his hands also lifted slightly, and Simon again began to talk about his aversion to close proximity. Rather than focus on the content, I asked him to momentarily put the narrative aside in order to focus his mindful attention exclusively on his hands and be aware of what "wants to happen" somatically. These small anticipatory movements, such as lifting of the hands, are evident in the minute physical gestures that are made in preparation for a larger movement (Ogden, Minton & Pain, 2006). Called "preparatory" or "intentional" movements, these involuntary movement adjustments occur just before a voluntary movement. As Bowlby (1982) states, "Intention movements are common in mammals, including man. They afford important clues whereby we judge the motives and likely behaviour of other people" (p. 99). Such movements are dependent upon the planned or voluntary movement for the form they take (Bouisset, 1991). I interpreted Simon's hand movement as possibly indicative of a defensive response (a "fight" response) associated with past trauma, emerging in barely perceptible physical movements of his hands that precede a larger defensive movement. These micro-movements are visible before the execution of a gross motor movement, and can take a variety of forms: a tiny crouch before a leap, a slight clenching of a fist before the strike, or an opening of a hand before a reach. These small movements provide cues to action sequences that "wanted to happen" but were typically not fully executed at the time of the trauma.

Once the therapist catches a glimpse of such a movement, as I did, the movement can be mindfully explored. I asked Simon what his hands might "want to do" and he described a physical feeling in his arms of wanting to push away. Note that this emerged from his awareness of his body, not as an idea or thought. I encouraged him to make that action, holding a pillow against Simon's hands for him to push against. It was important that Simon simply focus on his body in order to find a way to push that felt "right", and by executing an empowering defensive action, his anxiety decreased and the tension relaxed. Simon's internal locus of control was strengthened because he was the one in charge of how much pressure I should use in resisting his pushing with the pillow, what position to be in, how long to push, and so on. Through this exploration, Simon discovered the "right" distance between us, and also was able to mindfully execute a boundary-setting action in response to proximity, rather than the explosive violence he often experienced when people came near to him. The hope is that the resultant experience of regulated assertion would carry over to other elements of Simon's life. It should be noted that while Simon experienced relief and relaxation as he pushed away, this is not always the case. Often, when protective actions such as pushing away have incited the perpetrator to more violence in the past, these actions are abandoned, and executing them in the "safe" context of therapy can be terrifying. In such cases, clients need time, encouragement and practice to execute these actions.

Simon said he felt safe "being in control" of the distance between us, and I assured him that he was definitely "in charge." As our work proceeded, he repeatedly lamented about one woman he was particularly attracted to and wanted to approach, but could not. This discussion led us to another exploration of physical action in which we stood about fifteen feet apart, and Simon explored making a beckoning gesture to invite proximity between us. As he attempted to execute this proximity-seeking gesture, Simon averted his eyes, looking down. Proximity is fine-tuned by eye contact, bringing people closer or more distant. The eyes, like all non-verbal cues, change moment to moment. A sudden tightening or narrowing of the eyes might indicate pain, aversion, disagreement, suspicion or threat, while a widening of the eyes might signal excitement, surprise, or shock. Eye contact can be frightening for trauma survivors, and clients may be "beset by shame and anxiety and terrified by being judged and "seen" by the therapist" (Courtois, 1999, p. 190). I found myself imagining Simon as a boy, experiencing a desperate need for proximity, yet fearful of what he might see in the eyes of the other.

Simon found the beckoning action literally impossible to execute. Each time he tried, the action, which was intended as an invitation to approach him, morphed into an aggressive, challenging movement. Instead of a friendly signal intended to increase proximity between us, the gesture he made with his arms and hands was confrontational. He said the gesture was a challenge to fight, and his eyes met mine in a rather cold, defended stare as he lifted his chin. Simon had reported that his body became tense when he considered beckoning me closer, but as he made the confrontational gesture, he said, "There is no more tension. Because this is something I would do if I were calling someone over. A, it's a position of control, and B, that is only something I would do if I were provoking someone. I would be moving in. This is like I'm provoking someone." A different self-state had emerged to replace the one who, a few moments earlier, had wanted to explore proximity.

When attachment figures are also a threat to the child, as were Simon's parents, a confusing and contradictory set of behaviours ensues that can be conceptualised as the result of simultaneous or alternating stimulation of attachment and defence systems (Lyons-Ruth & Jacobvitz, 1999; Main & Morgan, 1996; Steele, Van der Hart & Nijenhuis, 2001; Van der Hart, et al., 2006). When the attachment system is stimulated, a person might instinctively seek proximity and engagement, but during proximity, which is perceived to be threatening, the defensive subsystems of flight, fight, freeze, hypoarousal/feigned death or submissive behaviours are mobilised. Therapists may be baffled by the paradoxical responses of their patients to relational contact. Despite Simon's stated wish to invite people "in" as he attempted to execute a beckoning action, an aggressive, defensive action emerged instead, representing two very different self-states and working models. Each seemed to predict markedly different outcomes from relational proximity. But these conflicting actions can be understood, given Simon's attachment history. As Bowlby (1973) states, the therapist "is striving jointly with the patient, to understand how the models on which the forecasts are based may have come into being" (p. 207). "During those inquiries it is often found that a model, currently active but at best of doubtful current validity, becomes reasonably or even completely intelligible when the actual experiences that the client has had in his day-to-day dealings with attachment figures during all his years of immaturity are known." (p. 207)

Simon reported, "I had a lot of bad and weird relationships when I invited someone in—it always turns bad." But he said he was willing to explore it with me, saying, "I feel safe with you, and I'm a lot stronger than you. And, I could take you down." Simon had studied boxing, and his strength and prowess was a source of safety for him. I asked him to be mindful of what happened inside if he just thought about inviting me closer, and Simon said he heard a voice inside saying, "What are you doing?" It seemed evident that two self-states, and two behavioural systems, with conflicting goals were activated. Bowlby (1973) states, "The behaviour to which the activation of one behavioural system leads may be highly compatible with the behaviour to which activation of another system leads; or it may be highly incompatible with it; or some parts of one may be compatible with some parts of the other, whilst other parts of each are incompatible with each other" (p. 97). We know that children with attachment trauma in their histories have grown up with attachment figures that might provoke extremes of low arousal (as in neglect) and high arousal (as in abuse) that tend to endure over time (Schore, 2007). Experiencing high sympathetic arousal—intense alarm, higher cortisol levels, and elevated heart rate—vacillating with increased dorsal vagal tone—slowed heart rate and shutdown (Schore, 2001)—these children, and later adults, are left with an inability to effectively auto- or interactively regulate. They suffer from rapid, dramatic, exhausting and confusing shifts of intense emotional states, from dysregulated fear, anger, or even elation, to despair, helplessness, shame, or flat affect. These affective biases might become enduring patterns of various self-states, some of which avoid interactive regulation, and some of which avoid auto- regulation, and most of which are good at neither.

Each self-state within Simon had its own working model, which they did not communicate to one another directly. As Bromberg (2012) confirms, "The felt otherness between one's *own states* becomes an alien 'thing' to be managed because it can no longer be contained as negotiable internal conflict that is mediated by self–other wholeness" (p. 274). Simon was unable to hold the differing "truths" of different self-states in his mind at the same time. He vacillated between his expressed desire to seek proximity and his habit of aggression that gave him a sense of safety and control.

Bowlby (1982) asserted that,

> … much of the work of treating an emotionally disturbed person can be regarded as consisting, first, of detecting the existence of influential models of which the client may be partially or completely unaware, and, second of inviting the client to examine the models disclosed and to consider whether they continue to be valid. (p. 205)

Exploring simple physical actions can bring forward a here-and-now experience of a variety of self-states and their working models that may be

> inhospitable and even adversarial, sequestered from one another as islands of 'truth,' each functioning as an insulated version of reality that protectively defines what is 'me' at a given moment and forcing other self states that are inharmonious with its truth to become 'not-me'. (Bromberg, 2010, p. 21)

When Simon explored the beckoning action, the self-state that had learned to inhibit that action became frightened and oppositional. Having made up its mind that others were never to be relied upon to respond to his need, this part of him believed seeking proximity to be a hopeless and even threatening action. New actions, like new words, can be viewed as threatening and adversarial by other self-states whose reality is challenged by such actions. Keep in mind that these actions are not simply physical exercises: they are rich with strong attachment-related emotions that were not regulated by the attachment figures in early childhood and/or with trauma-related emotions of terror and rage that accompany animal defences. Processing these actions and their affects can ultimately encourage self-states to get to know one another and increase the ease of transitions between states.

At a later point in our work, Simon reported that he could sense an emotional need for contact with others in his chest, but would override it with physical or mental activity. When he sensed this need, he said he either became very active or went to sleep. I suggested that he make physical contact with the place in his chest that had the need for emotional support, demonstrated by bringing my own hands gently to my own chest. A client's self-touch can be used to facilitate communication between different self-states. Touch brings sensitivity and awareness to a particular area of the body, thus often eliciting feelings, memories, etc. that are reflected in the body. When clients touch themselves, their awareness is naturally drawn to that area of the body, and the memories, images, beliefs, and feelings that are associated with that area, might begin to emerge.

Simon brought his hands to his chest in a sudden, and an aggressive, pushing motion, rather than in the gentle manner I had demonstrated.

Even so, it was a poignant and tender moment as Simon physically contacted the part of himself that held emotional need, and his words revealed the intensity of neglect, abuse, and pain this self-state had suffered. After a moment, Simon reported, "It feels like I'm, uh, I'm putting gauze down on a wound. Like you're pressing it in, like if someone's throat got ripped and you're trying to stop the blood flow … just keeping it alive." He went on to say, "I'm pushing more and more, it's the exact physical analogy, the blood flow inside is better and it kind of calms down. Making it last as long as possible." We spoke together about his connecting with this neglected, hurt part of himself, and I found myself moved by Simon's courage and the depth of his pain. I said, "It touches me because it feels that this part of you with normal human emotional need has been so wounded—it's barely been kept alive." At that very moment, Simon removed his hands from his chest. In retrospect, I believe that my overtly sharing in his pain was too much for him, or for parts of him, to integrate at the time. The interpersonal component was more than he could or was willing to address; he had done enough for the moment.

When Simon removed his hand so abruptly, I felt sad for the tender place inside him that he had abandoned with that withdrawal of his own touch. What I did not realise until later was that I also felt that he had abandoned me. Together we had been recognising the self-state in him, long neglected, which was needy, and when he abandoned that part of him, he also left me out on a limb, still wanting to attend to his long-ignored need. While I did not voice my disappointment, I am sure Simon or one of his self-states sensed it, and possibly felt that he had let me down, or disappointed me. He could have felt misunderstood, challenged, or even angry. Of course, all these reactions were most likely implicit remaining in the recesses of his unconscious but still exerting their effect on him and on us.

Therapy is always an uncertain dance of safety, and risk. Bromberg (2006) discussed the atmosphere of the therapeutic relationship as being "safe but not too safe." Simon and I were both implicitly feeling at least somewhat unsafe in our relationship, and together we would be compelled to navigate the risky terrain of working at our own regulatory boundaries. This would be challenging for us both because the unforeseeable dynamics between us would elicit self-states that wanted something from the other that would not be forthcoming. A self-state of mine wanted Simon to be willing and able to integrate the emotionally needy part of him; a self-state of Simon's needed me to allow and welcome his own pacing. These unspoken needs subtly threatened the safety we had established within our relationship. The implicit, elusive dance of what we enacted beneath the words felt vaguely familiar to me, and probably to Simon as well. It is primarily these implicit communications that lead to "safe surprises" (Bromberg, 2006) of relational negotiations that were neither intended nor predicted. Through the intimate encounters of the enactments between us, we would find that higher levels of organisation and integration would become possible.

Bromberg (2006) states,

> the road to the client's unconscious is always created nonlinearly by the analyst's own unconscious participation in its construction while he is consciously engaged in one way or another with a different part of the client's self. (p. 43)

Alongside the narrative, implicit encoding and decoding are taking place in a meaningful non-verbal conversation between the self-states of therapist and client. Encoding "involves an ability to emit accurate nonverbal messages about one's needs, feelings, and thoughts," while decoding "involves an ability to detect, accurately perceive, understand and respond appropriately to another person's nonverbal expressions of needs, interactions, feelings, thoughts, social roles" (Schachner, Shaver & Mikulincer, 2005, p. 148). The ongoing interactive process of encoding and decoding, reflected in shifts in movement and expression, shapes what happens within the relationship without conscious thought or intent. Note that implicit self-states of both client and therapist are engaged in this dance. It is through navigating the body-to-body, affect-laden conversations of multiple self-states, along with the verbal narrative, that the "safe surprises" (Bromberg, 2006) of relational negotiations can emerge.

Although I had been disappointed that Simon had truncated contact with his emotional need when he removed his hands from his chest, he later reported, "Whenever sort of a real stressful situation comes out, all this stress, doing that [covering the heart] is a very good means to self calm. I mean it's sort of like, I don't know, the tension kind of goes away, and I can start being rational again, and stop having negative thoughts, can have rational thoughts." Bowlby (1998) states that under certain circumstances the attachment system can be "rendered either temporarily or permanently incapable of being activated, and with it the whole range of feeling and desire that normally accompanies it is rendered incapable of being aroused" (p. 34). By targeting physical actions as sources of therapeutic action, Simon and I, together, had managed to not only discover and challenge his working models and arouse the feeling of emotional need but to also facilitate some communication between self-states. The action itself of covering the heart, as Simon described it, was something concrete that he could and did continue on his own, implicitly communicating a beginning acceptance of his emotional need to himself. The original wisdom of his body was revealed in his propensity to fight and refrain from proximity-seeking actions in order to protect himself and avoid any chances of a repeat of his early abuse. In spite of his history, Simon was able to explore new physical actions of connection and integration that challenged his outdated working models, and began to bring to life his own need. Through his courageous work, he began to cease being subjected to "old and unconscious stereotypes and to feel, to think, and to act in new ways" (Bowlby, 1988, p. 34).

References

Beebe, B. (2006). Co-constructing mother–infant distress in face-to-face interactions: Contributions of microanalysis. *Infant Observation, 9*(2): 151–164.
Bouisset, S. (1991). Relationship between postural support and intentional movement: biomechanical approach. *Archives Internationales de Physiologie, de Biochimie et de Biophysique, 99*: A77–A92.
Bowlby, J. (1982 [1969]). *Attachment: Attachment and Loss (Vol 1.)*. New York: Basic.
Bowlby, J. (1973). *Separation: Anxiety and Anger. Attachment and Loss (Vol 2.)*. New York: Basic.
Bowlby, J. (1988). *A Secure Base: Parent–Child Attachment and Healthy Human Development*. New York: Basic.
Bromberg, P. M. (2006). *Awakening the Dreamer: Clinical Journeys*. New Jersey: Analytic Press.
Bromberg, P. M. (2010). Minding the dissociative gap. *Contemporary Psychoanalysis, 46*(1): 19–31.
Bromberg, P. M. (2011). *The Shadow of the Tsunami and the Growth of the Relational Mind*. New York: Routledge.
Bromberg, P. M. (2012). Credo. *Psychoanalytic Dialogues, 22*(3): 273–278.
Chu, J. (1988). Ten traps for therapists in the treatment of trauma survivors. *Dissociation, 1*: 25–32.

Courtois, C. (2011 [1999]). *Healing the Incest Wound: Adult Survivors in Therapy* (2nd edn). New York: Norton.
Grigsby, J., & Stevens, D. (2000). *Neurodynamics of Personality*. New York, London: Guilford Press.
Kurtz, R. (1990). *Body-Centered Psychotherapy: The Hakomi Method: The Integrated Use of Mindfulness, Nonviolence, and the Body*. Mendocino, CA: Life Rhythm.
Kurtz, R. (2004). *Level 1 Handbook for the Refined Hakomi Method*. hakomi.com. [last accessed 4/01/2012].
Kurtz, R. (2010). Readings. hakomi.com/wp-content/uploads/2009/12/Readings-January-2010.pdf. [last accessed 3/12/2010].
Linehan, M. M. (1993). *Skills Training Manual for Treating Borderline Personality Disorder*. New York: Guilford Press.
Llinas, R. (2001). *I of the Vortex: From Neurons to Self*. Cambridge, MA: Massachusetts Institute of Technology Press.
Lyons-Ruth, K. (1998). Implicit relational knowing: its role in development and psychoanalytic treatment. *Infant Mental Health Journal, 19*: 282–289.
Lyons-Ruth, K., & Jacobvitz, D. (1999). Attachment disorganization: unresolved loss, relational violence, and lapses in behavioral and attentional strategies. In J. Cassidy & P. Shaver (Eds.), *Handbook of Attachment: Theory, Research, and Clinical Applications* (pp. 520–554). New York: Guilford Press.
Main, M., & Morgan, H. (1996). Disorganization and disorientation in infant strange situation behavior: Phenotypic resemblance to dissociative states. In: L. Michelson & W. J. Ray. (Eds.), *Handbook of Dissociation: Theoretical, Empirical, and Clinical Perspectives* (pp. 107–138). New York: Plenum Press.
Ogden, P. (2007). Beyond words: a clinical map for using mindfulness of the body and the organization of experience in trauma treatment. Paper presented at *Mindfulness and Psychotherapy Conference*. Los Angeles, CA: UCLA/Lifespan Learning Institute.
Ogden, P. (2009). Emotion, mindfulness and movement: expanding the regulatory boundaries of the window of tolerance. In: D. Fosha, D. Siegal, & M. Solomon (Eds.), *The Healing Power of Emotion: Perspectives from Affective Neuroscience and Clinical Practice* (pp. 204–231). New York: Norton.
Ogden, P. (In press). Beyond conversation in sensorimotor psychotherapy: embedded relational mindfulness. In: V. M. Follette, D. Rozelle, J. W. Hopper, D. I. Rome, & J. Briere (Eds.), *Contemplative Methods in Trauma Treatment: Integrating Mindfulness and other Approaches*. New York: Guilford Press.
Ogden, P., & Minton, K. (2000). Sensorimotor psychotherapy: One method for processing traumatic memory. *Traumatology, 6*(3): 1–20.

Ogden, P., Minton, K., & Pain, C. (2006). *Trauma and the Body: A Sensorimotor Approach to Psychotherapy*. New York: Norton.

Piaget, J. (1962). *Play, Dreams, and Imitation in Childhood*. New York: Norton.

Schachner, D., Shaver, P., & Mikulincer, M. (2005). Patterns of nonverbal behavior and sensitivity in the context of attachment relationships. *Journal of Nonverbal Behavior*, 29(3): 141–169.

Schore, A. (1994). *Affect Regulation and the Origin of the Self: The Neurobiology of Emotional Development*. Hillsdale, New Jersey: Lawrence Erlbaum Associates.

Schore, A. (2001). The effects of early relational trauma on right brain development, affect regulation, and infant mental health. *Infant Mental Health Journal*, 22: 201–269.

Schore, J., & Schore A. N. (2007). Modern attachment theory: the central role of affect regulation in development and treatment. *Clinical Social Work Journal*, 36: 9–20.

Siegel, D. (1999). *The Developing Mind*. New York: Guilford Press.

Steele, K., Van der Hart, O., & Nijenhuis, E. R. S. (2001). Dependency in the treatment of Complex PTSD and Dissociative Disorder patients. *Journal of Trauma and Dissociation*, 2: 79–116.

Tronick, E. Z. (2009). Multilevel meaning making and dyadic expansion of consciousness theory: the emotional and the polymorphic and polysemic flow of meaning. In: D. Fosha, D. Siegel, & M. Solomon (Eds.), *The Healing Power of Emotion: Affective Neuroscience, Development and Clinical Practice* (pp. 86–110). New York: Norton.

Tulving, E., & D. L. Schacter (1990). Priming and human memory systems. *Science*, 247: 301–306.

Van der Hart, O., Nijenhuis, E., & Steele, K. (2006). *The Haunted Self*. New York: Norton.

Van der Kolk, B. (2006). Series Editor's Foreword, in P. Ogden, K. Minton, & C. Pain, *Trauma and the Body: A Sensorimotor Approach to Psychotherapy*, (pp. xviii–xxvi). New York: Norton.

Van der Kolk, B. A., McFarlane, A., & Weisaeth, L. (1996). *Traumatic Stress: The Effects of Overwhelming Experience on Mind, Body and Society*. New York: Guilford Press.

CHAPTER SIX

Touching trauma: working relationally and safely with the unboundaried body

Orit Badouk Epstein

Touch has a memory (John Keats)

As humans we exist with a rich tapestry of relational patterns, in which each individual is unique. Most of our clients have some form of traumatic experience, where their early relationships were either avoidant, ambivalent, or disruptive and unpredictable. Their environment did not provide them with the secure and safe holding they needed.

According to Alison Miller "The research evidence has not changed in the past fifty years: the factor that matters most in successful psychotherapy is the bond between the client and the therapist" (Miller, 2012, p. 209).

In this chapter I'd like to reflect on my personal approach to relational psychotherapy, which I hope can demonstrate various ways to understand meaningful attachment relationships in a wider context.

In the same way as a computer programmer, an engineer or a scientist will always try to work on ways of making improvements within their own field, similarly as an attachment-based psychotherapist I see my role to always try to find ways that will enhance my connection with my clients, particularly when we know that we are often most touched by actions of human kindness that stand outside the conventional box of relatedness.

Before building the therapeutic alliance, the first and foremost aspect of human relatedness is to feel safe. Safety is our primal need. It is the backbone of a trusting relationship. Without first feeling safe with another person, nothing can proceed healthily. This may take time, particularly with traumatised clients, who will watch every move and scan every word that you as their therapist say, to see whether or not you are trustworthy, believing that it is most likely you are not, but at the same time hoping desperately that you will prove otherwise.

Establishing external boundaries, such as keeping to the length of a session, the contract around fees, the issue of confidentiality and receiving regular supervision are very necessary. However, my emphasis is on how to improve the therapeutic alliance; how my client and I in the intersubjective space between us can regulate our feelings better with each other. I will therefore focus more on the issues of what I call "internal boundaries" or, more accurately, trusting the relationship with the authentic flow of the transference/countertransference, when with attunement we are able to differentiate between what is helpful and what is unhelpful to us and others. In trusting the transference I often leave it to the client to let me know what they need.

As therapists we often find that what a client communicates verbally is not always congruent with his or her body's story. So what can we do with the bodily aspects of the client when they enter our consulting rooms? The body that self harms; the body that never washes to keep you at bay; the body that always hurts without knowing why; the body that shivers even on a hot summer's day; the body that jumps and is startled at the slightest of noises; the body that picks its skin, nails and hair; the body that smells of strong detergents; the body that has lost somebody; the body that is disembodied or the body that is no body.

In a recent interview the writer Tony Morrison said that she had dedicated her latest book *Home* to her son Slade, who had died recently and in the face of whose death she found herself wordless. She could not work. She could barely speak and didn't want to hear comforting words from others.

> What do you say? There really are no words for that. There really aren't. Somebody tries to say, 'I'm sorry, I'm so sorry'. People say that to me. There is no language for it. Sorry doesn't do it. I think

you should just hug people and mop their floor or something. (*Guardian Weekend*, 2012, p. 17)

In his book *Attachment & Loss* (1997), Bowlby asserted that bonding between infant and caregiver arose from a primary motivation to attach, which entailed intimate physical contact and clinging behaviour.

Following on from Bowlby, in 1958 Harry Harlow, an American scientist who was greatly intrigued by the concept of love, conducted a series of experiments on young monkeys. One of them was to demonstrate the importance of contact comfort. He separated a monkey from its mother, giving the young monkey two dummy mothers: one model was made of wire with a milk bottle attached to it and the other was made of a soft cloth. The monkey rarely stayed with the wire feeding-dummy and clearly preferred cuddling with the softer contact model, especially if it was frightened. His conclusion was that the need for contact overrode the need for food.

When my own children had to have a vaccination during babyhood, I insisted on holding them while the nurse gave them their injection. The nurse was amazed that they didn't cry at all. This experience has made me think that touch isn't only there to function as a holding mechanism but also has the power to reduce pain.

In his report for the World Health Organization on *Maternal Care and Mental Health*, John Bowlby (1952) describes the importance of touch as essential to human development, critical to the health and well-being of children as well as having a capacity for promoting healing.

My son was born prematurely at thirty-two weeks. He was separated from me and lay in an incubator for ten days. On reunion, I held him intensely for the first six months, as the skin to skin contact helped his body heal and better integrate after his birth trauma. At six months the doctors could not tell that he had been born prematurely.

Attunement through touch helps babies regulate breathing, decreases stress hormones, regulates body temperature, stabilises heart rate and enhances their sleep patterns. In Israel a charity named "Hug Me" works closely with abandoned babies in hospital. They recruit volunteers to come and spend at least six hours a day physically holding, massaging and rocking a baby until the babies are three months old and are allocated to an adoptive family. I'd like to reiterate that touch attunement is not the responsibility of the biological mother alone, any caregiver can provide this as long as it is consistent, attuning and loving so that one can give the baby the security he or she needs. It can also be argued that touch attunement is couched within a cultural context. I have heard people say: "the reason it works for you is because you are from a different culture, where touch is more accepted and integrated." Like many other cultural generalisations this can be used as a defence and a way of distancing the matter further.

According to Winnicott, a securely attached baby is one who feels ownership of the mother's body where a sensitive and soothing parental response is available and predictable. On the other hand for the insecurely attached child, touch is absent when necessary or inappropriately intrusive, sexualised, withheld, or abusive in other ways. Experiences of touch will get recorded in the brain and if misattuned or intrusive will manifest in many dysfunctional ways later in life. If children don't get healthy touch they are more vulnerable to people who are acting in a predatory way and who could ultimately harm them. Lack of safe touch to the body during the formative period of life is one of the primary causes of violent behaviour in adults (Prescott, 1975).

Neuroscientific research has ample evidence to demonstrate the importance of non-verbal communication and its long lasting effects on the body and mind and subsequent behaviour. We now know that when we become familiar with someone, touch allows a general capacity to expand ourselves as part of a social system. Brain activity research shows that touch releases chemical responses including a decrease in stress hormones such as cortisol, catecholamines, norepinephrine, epinephrine and increases serotonin and dopamine levels, which all help in decreasing depression (Perry, 2010).

So why is it that touch remains such a taboo subject in the psychoanalytic psychotherapy setting? Starting with Freud, traditional psychoanalysis sees touch as a hindrance to analysis and the cure of neurosis. We know that great clinicians such as Ferenczi, Jung, R. D. Laing and others exploited touch in their practice and therefore the use of touch has been shunned by psychotherapists ever since, viewing any non-erotic touch as the first step on the slippery slope towards a sexual relationship. However we also know that Bowlby, Winnicott, Balint and Margaret Little worked effectively with touch in their practice.

In his last interview with Virginia Hunter in 1990 Bowlby said:

> As a male therapist, one has to be careful about using touch, but that doesn't mean to say I haven't used touch because I have … Touch

is something which is both very important and full of pitfalls. It's a difficult subject, to do systematic research on for reasons we've discussed and there is very little systemic research in point of fact and that's a pity. (Hunter, 1991, p. 168)

Touch can be the most powerful form of communication throughout the course of one's life, holding immense potential for use, as well as misuse, for healing as well as for harm. It's important to acknowledge "that a therapist's attitude towards touch and their tendency to sexualize touch are the key factors in contributing to sexual misconduct rather than touch itself" (Zur & Nordmarken, 2011, p. 15). Body attunement means that in trusting the countertransference effectively the therapist is able to use the right touch in the right place at the right time.

In her book *The Power of Countertransference* Karen Maroda (2009) wrote:

> I refuse to believe that most therapists are so inherently unstable or self indulgent that if they are encouraged to use their intuition and emotion in addition to their intellect in a responsible manner the only result will be wild and destructive. (Maroda, 2009, p. 82)

I use touch as an adjunct to talking therapy and use the following types of touch:

Consolation touch—Holding of the hands or shoulders of a client or providing a comforting hug usually constitutes this kind of supportive or soothing touch. It is most often done in response to grief, deep sorrow, distress, anguish, or upset. This is one of the most important forms of touch and is likely to enhance the therapeutic alliance.

Grounding or reorienting touch—This form of touch is intended to help clients reduce anxiety or dissociation. By employing a touch to the arm or hand, it usually involves helping a client to be aware of his or her physical body. It can also be done by helping a client touch some fabric or by leading them to touch their own bodies, for example encouraging them to stroke their arm.

Indirect touch—Examples of this type of touch are gently covering the traumatised body with a blanket, giving a teddy bear or a hot water bottle to a client. Similarly, transitional objects can often be used as a tool to mediate touch.

Reassuring touch—This type of touch is often done at the end of a session with a warm hug or a shake of a hand.

To demonstrate my use of touch, I will now discuss a few clinical examples starting with a depressed client.

Claire

Claire is a high-achieving professional who is in her thirties. On arrival to therapy she looked like an underdeveloped pubescent. Her depression was chronic. Her loneliness and failed relationships with both men and women pointed to her terror of intimacy. She also suffered from regular panic attacks and back pain. The minute she sat on the couch she burst into floods of tears and cried inconsolably. When I asked her what was hurting her, she had no idea why she was feeling the way she did.

Claire's attachment history revealed no physical or sexual trauma. Her father was an absent academic leaving her with her mum and two older siblings. As a child and as an adult Claire always felt excluded and second best most of the time. Her mother was controlling, critical, and withholding, yet Claire would often yearn for her mother's tea and cookies as a symbol of their connection with each other. Her neediness for her mother was like that of a clingy, preoccupied child who could not recognise that the proximity she was seeking from her mother's emotional unavailability was the root cause of her depression.

Balint (1959) said, "By clinging one gets farther and farther away from the satisfaction of the original need, which was to be held safe" (Balint, 1959, p. 120).

Claire spent most of her first six months in therapy sobbing uncontrollably; her grief was palpable, her body slouched and her limbs looked floppy. In my countertransference with Claire I felt a huge sense of loss and a lack of holding in her upbringing. This was communicated not so much through her narrative, as she often idealised her childhood, but more through her body. Her child-like body felt as if it was falling apart at the slightest sign of stress. Claire's high academic achievements had come to a halt as her anxiety levels shot up and she would wake up every morning with knots in her stomach, dreading the day ahead.

Making a link between her upbringing and her anxious self, at times, felt a bit of a challenge, she persisted in telling me: "They did their best, I don't think that me being anxious is due to my childhood."

In Alice Miller's (2006) book *The Body Never Lies*, she describes many examples from her experience as an analyst that illustrate her contention that what the mind is unable to recall is remembered in the body.

At the European Society for Trauma and Dissociation (ESTD) 2011 conference, a child psychotherapist from the Netherlands described children who come from families where they have developed avoidant attachment patterns as suffering from "Silent Trauma". Although Claire had patterns of preoccupied ambivalent attachment it was also very avoidant. Her affluent upbringing lacked adequate emotional responsiveness, and had left her narrative deprived of the language of emotion, not knowing why she felt the way she did. Claire is an academic who is used to intellectualising everything. However, offering her intellectual interpretations whilst witnessing her in this regressive state, constantly crying, felt more like misattunement than a helpful intervention.

I moved gently over and sat next to her and simply held her in my arms for long periods during the session. Using this gentle holding with a few reassuring words, Claire's body gradually started to feel and become stronger. Her silent trauma was transformed into a cohesive narrative that enabled her to realise that the cold, withholding and controlling mothering she received had made her a high achiever, yet inhibited her emotional maturation process. Claire's relationship with men verged on exploitation. A child who has been regularly controlled by her environment would hardly learn to say "no" to another.

Her mother's critical voice regularly invaded her body and penetrated her mind, all of which made her feel deeply unsupported and confused. With me holding her both emotionally and physically, Claire soon began to mourn the profound emotional deprivation she had learnt to repress and dissociate from. Within a year, Claire's excessive crying had greatly subsided as well as her panic attacks and depression. Her back pains have also quieted down completely.

In her recent book *Healing the Unimaginable*, Alison Miller (2012) wrote:

> Touch is a complicated issue in the field of psychotherapy and especially so with this client group. Stephan Ray, one of my early

teachers about ritual abuse said that he thought it was abusive not to touch clients who have been so massively neglected and abused. (Miller, 2012, p. 219)

Freddie

Freddie is a male survivor of ritual abuse and mind control. Freddie was sexually, physically and emotionally abused from birth until the age of sixteen. He suffered serious abuse by multiple perpetrators, no wonder then that in order to survive he had developed multiple parts.

When I watched Freddie's body jolting, jerking, shaking, stammering and screaming whilst recovering horrific memories and flashbacks of childhood torture and abuse, it made me feel almost inhuman to not hold his traumatised body. Freddie's horrendous abuse had left his deprived child parts desperately yearning for safe touch and nurture. However, these parts would often get muddled up and confused with the severely sexually and violent abused parts of himself.

As result of his abusive past, Freddie's traumatised body had developed Myalgic Encephalomyelitis (ME) and many other ailments. When he sat in therapy sessions his body appeared extremely tense. He nervously picked the skin around his finger nails and his toes barely touched the floor. His discomfort and awkwardness about his body was very noticeable.

For many clients who have been sexually abused, touch might cause anxiety and dysregulation at the start of therapy, but in the long run it will often create a sense of safety and help integrate the body and mind. In trying to model what secure attachment is meant to be like I felt it was helpful for Freddie's neglected and abused body to be introduced to the experience of safe, non-invasive and appropriate touch.

Gradually, as our alliance progressed, I asked little Freddie for his permission to gently hold his finger while his body went through the experience in the present of his past traumas. Being accustomed to being in a hyper aroused fight/flight state, his body froze. He then declined my offer and said: "no we are not sure". Rejecting touch is as important as being touched. By saying "no" to another person, the client can assert his right to be touched. This will help him to further integrate and gain autonomy over his body and mind.

In working with clients who have been diagnosed with DID (Dissociative Identity Disorder), as well as listening to the countertransference we need to be aware of the traumatic transference such as when one part communicates one need while another part may resent it.

A few weeks after this, during one of our intense sessions, "little Freddie" reached out his index finger to me; gradually stretching to a full palm he clung tightly onto my hand.

Freddie's early encounters with touch had been mostly sadistic and sexual. The intense sexual abuse Freddie had suffered at the hands of his family and many other cult members from birth had left him and his abused body exposed, boundary-less, and extremely confused. This meant that we had to go through many sexual re-enactments. On one occasion while sobbing in my arms, a part self-state emerged feeling confused and looked at me saying: "I was convinced that we were going to end up in bed, I don't understand why we are not in bed." These moments felt both compulsive and painful, often leaving Freddie feeling he was a disgusting and unworthy human being, riddled with shame and guilt.

In the film *Shame* directed by Steve McQueen (2011), McQueen depicts shame and humiliation as being deeply buried under guilt, and being at the forefront of addiction. Shame means that you feel bad for what or who you actually are. Shame sometimes arises from being used in an unacceptable or degrading manner, such as the shame about feeling physical/sexual excitement whilst being molested. The tormented addict's tendency to defend against shame is to numb and forget the pain of the haunting memories and flashbacks of their abused childhood. Shame is a painful emotion because it involves self-loathing and critical judgement of oneself that leads to feelings of humiliation, inadequacy, and isolation.

Freddie had no idea about what a healthy, nurturing relationship felt like. One of his parts was a sex addict: a hunter and seducer who regularly watched pornography and paid for sex, who, unless he seduced a woman, felt that he was unworthy and emasculated. This part was relentless in the first year of therapy; regularly attempting seduction during the sessions preventing any meaningful attachment happening. Holding the boundaries safely, time and again in a non-shaming or humiliating voice, I reiterated to Freddie that his sexual trauma had violated his basic need for healthy boundaries and appropriate touch. Children are not supposed to have sex with their parents or anyone else. Safe touch from a caregiver is meant to be soothing and help regulate feelings rather than arouse them. Little Freddie deserved to be introduced to healthy, safe touch. Without modelling safe touch, I felt Freddie would continue to objectify people, particularly women, and have a tendency to dominate and exploit them. My journey with Freddie continues to be a remarkable one, his recovery towards integration is rewarding to us both. He has given me his permission to publish an extract from a recent article he wrote:

> Now thanks to working with my therapist for three years, the little boy's been acknowledged and loved with an understanding, deep empathy and a safe touch; her impact was immediate and for the first time in his life he felt safe. The little parts became quickly attached to her, other parts are taking longer. In her unique way she checks that the little parts are okay, because she knows they hold the key to healing. She doesn't judge or criticise the sex-searcher who is not aware of little parts' needs, instead she encourages me to "trust the process" and will throw a useful gem from time to time:
>
> "You're too lovely just to fuck", she says. It's a clever comment because it addresses different parts within me; there is still conflicted response to hearing it. I nod in agreement, wanting to believe her more than I do, but the word lovely is winning by a hand today.

Freddie no longer suffers from ME or sex addiction and is currently in an intimate relationship with a woman.

Touch must always remain a choice, and is something that we as therapists cannot impose on the client. Nor is it meant to gratify our own needs. When in the countertransference I feel that touch might help healing, I will always ask the client's permission.

Miranda

"When the need for touch remains unsatisfied, abnormal behaviour will result." (Montagu, 1971 p. 46)

Miranda had been diagnosed with so called "schizoid affective disorder". To me though, her symptoms were of severe dissociation and detachment. Miranda was significantly overweight and rarely washed. Her body odour kept people at bay. On her neck she has a tattoo saying: "Back Off" in gothic script.

On her arrival in therapy she sat and stared at the floor, rarely making eye contact. Sometimes she mumbled incoherent things; sometimes she said that there were aliens inside her who didn't like coming to therapy. Her reluctance to talk about her abuse was stronger than anything. When she finally shed a few tears after two years in therapy, I asked her: "Would you like me to hold your hand?" She replied angrily: "Back off".

I gave Miranda some crayons and paper to help some of her non-verbal parts communicate. She often drew the sexual abuse and torture she endured at the hands of a number of men and women, all of whom were members of her family.

Touch was not an option for Miranda. She found any physical touch to be excruciating; she would shudder after the slightest brush against her skin on the Underground. This type of defence is called armouring (also a form of PTSD), which happens when the body makes a shield out of muscles to protect the bones and internal organs as a result of physical abuse—it was not safe for Miranda to be touched by me or anyone else. One of the reasons she was so terrified of trusting me was because of her regular contact with her abusive family. Keeping Miranda safe, at the moment, is my main priority; until she learns to separate from the attachment to her abusers our alliance will, of necessity, remain pretty much limited.

Bee

"Among all the senses touch stands paramount." (Montagu, 1986, p. 17)

Bee is a person who has been diagnosed with dissociative identity disorder (DID) with a highly functioning apparently normal personality (ANP), who has survived chilling and sadistic abuse by her mother, and violence and sexual abuse from her father and cult members. She is an extremely creative and bright person. Her creativity has enabled her to survive rape and torture. The internal world she created for herself was highly resourceful and her compulsive self-reliance, for example, found her a way of caring for the young parts of herself. Through reading parenting books Bee has developed an internal good mother who replaced the abusive mother, comforting Bee's young selves, who were usually terrified at night and found it hard to fall asleep.

At the beginning of therapy, Bee's silence during most of the session was overwhelming; I remember very clearly how in my countertransference I felt I wanted to cry. I later understood why. Bee's sadistic mother told her that she never cried as a baby because she was never picked up. Bee was not allowed to cry. She therefore learnt to cry and sob internally, without tears. Her crying was mute. She would wipe her invisible tears with her own handkerchief. As a toddler, Bee hadn't been allowed soft toys, or any form of transitional objects to help her comfort herself. She wasn't allowed to suck her thumb or even have a nap during the day. Her mother would often remove her duvet and leave her to freeze by leaving the window open during winter nights. Very much like Harlow's traumatised monkeys, Bee would often rock herself sitting on her bed whilst secretly patting her own eyebrow as this was the only "transitional object" available to her. To watch Bee in distress was very painful; she often arrived to the session just wearing a T-shirt on a cold winter's night, and sat on the couch with her body curled up, her feet not touching the floor, whilst silently crying and repeatedly rubbing one of her eyebrows.

Bee's mother hated her daughter's body and regularly insulted parts of her body, in particular her hands. On arrival to therapy Bee would cover her hands and look at them with sheer disgust. She would say: "They are claws, they are not mine they belong to her, she owns them". Bee's phobia of touch was stronger than anyone I knew. She often warned me, "We don't do touch, don't you dare touch us. Touch is disgusting, we are disgusting". Her body was always tense and in a fight/flight mode, just waiting to be attacked. She would jump at the slightest noise from the street and freeze at the sound of a car door slamming.

Bee's body was locked in a double bind; I felt that her young parts, who had spent hours naked, frozen, and shivering, sitting on a cold floor, were yearning for safe touch and a warm hug, yet her abused and tense body knew that touch was the most dangerous thing for them.

At first, I placed a teddy bear on the couch as well as a blanket. For the majority of the first year, Bee would push the teddy away from her and cover it up. I remember feeling a sense of relief when Bee, for the first time, reached out for the tissue box in my therapy room. As time went by, Bee's younger parts would appear regularly shaking and shivering, feeling terrified yet mute. I reached out for the blanket and covered her traumatised body. Bee's young parts self gave me a grateful look and started talking about what happened to them. In another session, when feeling a bit safer, Bee reached out for the teddy and cuddled it for most of the session.

One of her parts would often protest, "Feeling is dangerous; you are making us feel we don't like it". Nevertheless, as time passed, Bee talked more and looked less frightened. However, her hands remained hidden—always tucked away somewhere. The humiliation and sadistic bullying her hands and body had endured from her psychotic parents had made a part of her split off. This part was called "Shame".

> Chronically traumatised individuals almost always experience a devastating sense of shame of what has happened to them; the kind of shame goes far beyond healthy bounds. It is a chronic, pervasive and sustained experience as an utter failure, a flawed and defective human being. (Boon, Steel & Van der Hart, 2011, p. 289)

During one session, while Bee's head was deeply hunched into her body and she was constantly pinching and hiding her palms away, I symbolically took "shame" into my arms whilst rocking her, telling her that none of this was her fault and that there was nothing wrong with her beautiful hands. Bee slowly lifted her face. For the first time I could actually hear her crying and see her tears roll down; I offered my hand to her, hesitantly. Bee reached out with her index finger towards me. I held her finger in my hands, seconds later she opened up both her hands whilst holding my hand, this time with a smile.

> The skin is the most important organ system of the body, because like any other senses, a human being cannot survive without the physical and behavioural functions performed by the skin. (Montagu, 1971, p. 17).

When I first touched Bee's hand her skin felt terribly dry, hard, and brittle; her whole body was shaking and felt very tense. Today, Bee's hands are well integrated into her body and her skin is smooth. She is more at ease with herself, and her feet rest solidly on the floor.

Conclusion

As Toni Morrison (2012) said, when words are not enough and where there is no language to console such sorrow, touching with empathy might help alleviate pain. Touch attunement is meant to provide a much needed preverbal response to the client, through preverbal communication. In particular, touch is most effective when the attachment trauma began in infancy. In trusting the countertransference, using empathic touch not only provides a means for the therapist to maximise and enhance the interpersonal encounters inherent in the treatment, but can actually help ease pain and lift depression. Touching empathically must be done with the client's consent and should never gratify the therapist's needs. Regular supervision is the way to ensure that the client's safety is always maintained.

References

Balint, M. (1968). *The Basic Fault: Therapeutic Aspects of Regression*. London: Tavistock.

Boon, S., Steel, K., & Van der Hart, O. (2011). *Coping with Trauma Related Dissociation: Skills Training for Patients and Therapists*. New York: Norton.

Bowlby, J. (1952). *Maternal Care and Mental Health*. Geneva: World Health Organization.

Bowlby, J. (1997 [1969]). *Attachment: Attachment & Loss, Vol. 1*. London: Pimlico.

Brockes, E. (2012). Toni Morrison: I want to feel what I feel. Even if it's not happiness. *Guardian Weekend*, 14 March p. 17. Available at: www.guardian.co.uk.

Fosshage, J. L. (2000). The meanings of touch in psychoanalysis: A time for reassessment. *Psychoanalytic Inquiry, 20*(1): 21–43.

Harlow, H. (1958). The nature of love. *American Psychologist, 13*: 673–685.

Hunter, V. (1991). John Bowlby: An interview. *Psychoanalytic Review, 78*: 159–175.

Keats, J. (1994). Lines to Fanny. In: *The Complete Poems of John Keats* (p. 418). Ware: Wordsworth.

Maroda J. K. (2009). *The Power of Counter-transference*. New York: Routledge.

Miller, A. (2006). *The Body Never Lies: The Lingering Effects of Hurtful Parenting*. London: Norton.

Miller, A. (2012). *Healing the Unimaginable*. London: Karnac.

Montagu, A. (1986). *Touching: The Human Significance of the Skin*. New York: Harper & Row.
Perry, D. B., & Szlavitz, M. (2010). *Born for Love*. New York: Harper Collins.
Prescott, J. (1975). Body pleasure and the origins of violence, *The Futurist*, (*April*) 64–67.
Zur, O., & Nordmarken, N. (2011). *To Touch or not to Touch: Exploring the Myth of Prohibition On Touch In Psychotherapy And Counseling*. www.zurinstitute.com/touchintherapy.html [last accessed 30/09/2013].

CHAPTER SEVEN

The body I want: a psychotherapy with a disabled man

Mark Linington

A substantial part of my work as a psychotherapist has been with people with learning disabilities, both privately and in the National Health Service. Often these are people who have impaired bodies and sometimes additional difficulties communicating in words. People with learning disabilities can be ill-regarded, sometimes experience bad treatment from others, and be viewed as not at all suitable for psychotherapeutic help. Yet, in a passing reference to disability, Bowlby (1969) in his first volume on attachment says,

> To achieve his set-goal of proximity to mother any and all locomotory skills at a child's disposal are likely to be called upon. He will crawl, shuffle, walk, or run. If he is grossly deficient in locomotory equipment, for example as a result of thalidomide, he will still achieve his end, even if it means rolling. (Bowlby, 1969, p. 248)

People with disabilities, I may hardly need to say, have the same attachment needs and desires as other people in society, although these needs and desires may sometimes be communicated through different behaviours. I hope reflecting on psychotherapy with people with disabilities can help us think about some important issues for the work of all psychotherapy. Issues can become explicit in psychotherapy with someone with a disability that may remain less manifest in the psychotherapy of other people. In my work with Peter, this has been especially true about the significance of the body in clinical work.

I want a body

"I want a body. I want a different body. I want your body." This is what Peter said to me after two years of twice weekly attachment-based psychotherapy. In this period of our work, we had been thinking together, almost in every session, about his disability—a rare congenital disorder called Arthrogryposis that affected him physically and mentally. This was a time in the work together of growing grief; a grief that we had just begun to touch after some considerable time of building a secure enough relational base between us. When Peter said this to me—a liminal moment that brought our bodies into the work in a new, more mutually intersubjective way—I thought of his body afresh and felt more aware of my own body-self being there with him. This had become a more two-body therapy. I found myself looking at parts of my body—especially at my legs that were not disabled like his. I thought in his desire for my body, something different about his own body was emerging and being expressed—not just explicitly in his words, but in his entire implicit demeanour.

I noticed how he seemed to hold himself more upright and look at me in a way that felt more authentic. I wanted to recognise this new embodied relational him. I held his gaze and repeated the words he had said to me. Yet, also in my looking, I noticed that actually to look took me some effort—to see his body and take it in; I wanted to turn away my gaze. I realised that I could not manage to view the whole of his body—that I tended to the parts of him that did not seem disabled. In Peter's desire, a deep relational pain, an implied acknowledgement of a lack—there being something *wanting*—was also being expressed between us. This attachment trauma—this lack—that was being avoidantly regulated; that I was regulating avoidantly in the turning away of my gaze—was perhaps a complementary re-enactment of a parental relationship.

Furthermore, I was aware of having a complex set of feelings and thoughts stirred around inside me—a discomfort that I experienced working around in my gut. As I experienced this feeling, I noticed Peter shifting around his body in his wheelchair. Something was happening inside his body. I said, "When we talk about the body you want, it seems like you have a feeling inside". He said, "I don't feel right in myself Mark. My body's all wrong. I want your body".

I felt uncomfortable him desiring my body in this way. I found it too possessing, too guilt-inducing; a sort of threat to my subjectivity. In his wanting, I felt he was trying to pull me too close into him. There was an intrusive feeling of sexual charge. I felt anxious about this presence of a not so implicit sexual desire—an anxiety which had a root, I think, in the fact that Peter had been raped by a man, when he was a teenager and had in later life become involved in a number of relationships with both men and women that had involved ongoing sexual abuse.

First meeting

In my mind, I made a connection to my first meeting with Peter, two years previously, when I had a not dissimilar swirl of potent and discomforting feelings and thoughts. First meetings often evoke a response in me that can be useful for understanding the relational issues and traumas of the person coming to see me. Over the years, rather than dissociating in the anxiety of the moment, I have tried to pay more careful attention to what happens to me when I meet someone—the images that come to mind, the feelings I experience, the responses of my body, and the way I behave. These all seem helpful in beginning to understand aspects of the relational models, marked by the traumas and attachment difficulties, with which the person is coming to the encounter. Peter was early for our first session; but when I went out to meet him at the beginning of our time, he was outside smoking a cigarette. As he came into the waiting area, I was immediately and acutely struck by the beautiful masculinity of his face. I noticed how strong, muscular and attractive his upper body appeared. I took this in—more than his being in a wheelchair, which he moved towards me with a confident proficiency—holding out his arm for some time, before he came within reach of shaking my hand. I thought of my son raising his arms, as a signal, wanting to be picked up. I noticed how firm and warm Peter's hand felt. I had a feeling of longing for the muscular comfort of a father's caregiving body. Mixed in with this overall pleasurable—and somewhat father-young boy experience—I had an intruding unwelcome thought about the dirtiness of this masculine warmth. I felt contaminated. I wanted to keep my own hand separate from myself. I could wash it later and return it to its normal state, when it could once again become part of me. I felt guilty for feeling so stereotypically sullied. I noticed his small legs, in trousers too big for him. He held my gaze directly, smiling in a too broad, perhaps-handicapped, way (Sinason, 2010) and said an ebullient hello, introducing himself and using my name frequently.

We went to the consulting room. In the room he shifted his body around, and moved his wheelchair into different positions, as though he could not find the right proximity to me. As I looked at his legs and thought how childlike they seemed, like those of a seven-year-old, I found myself wondering about whether his sexual organs were normal. I felt a rush of nausea at this abusive-feeling juxtaposition. I had somehow put together a seven year-old and adult's sexual desire. He said he had something to talk about with me and began talking like we were already in an intimate relationship.

Referral

Peter referred himself for psychotherapy, because he was having difficulties in his relationship with his partner, Ann, who also had a physical and learning disability. They lived separately and had been in a romantic relationship for eight years. The difficulties Peter described—with a look of imploring on his face—were that she was making horrible remarks and doing things to his body that hurt him. He said he did not know what to do about this. She was putting her hand over his mouth, saying that she did not love him and that she wanted to marry other men. With some struggle and a pained expression on his face, he said she was calling him a "fucking spastic". He said that he loved her and he did not understand why she was doing these things. He wanted my advice on what to do about these difficulties. Every now and again he would stop and say: "So what should I do, Mark, what do you think the answer is?" He told me they had recently begun a course as a couple, training them to offer sex education courses to other people with disabilities. He said they enjoyed the sexual aspect of their relationship; but he also hinted that Ann was not always completely happy about it. He could not elaborate on this.

I met Peter for two initial assessment sessions. He said that he had discussed things with Ann and she had agreed that they should have some help. He thought they could go to therapy as a couple. I wondered if Relate might be a helpful place to go. Peter said that he thought this was a good idea—although, I also sensed that he was hurt by a feeling of rejection by me. He asked me to help him do this and I contacted Relate to make a referral.

In the week that I made this referral, Peter went to the police because Ann had attacked him with scissors across his chest and in his genital area, while they were having sex together. Although his injuries had not been life threatening, they were serious, and if Ann had not stopped what she was doing, Peter might have died. The police arrested Peter's partner; she was cautioned and released.

Soon afterwards, Peter contacted me and asked to come back to see me following this incident. Again, I felt guilty—like my cutting him off had led to the cutting attack on his body. I felt uncomfortable that our attachment had begun in such an ambivalent way and was marred by such violence. For the first few months of our work we talked about this incident, in which social workers, police and psychiatric services were involved. Although advised to stay away from his partner by the police, Peter continued to try and have contact with her—although he denied this for quite a while. He was seen on the CCTV at the entrance of Ann's house, dragging himself along the floor while she held the door open for him, so that he could leave his wheelchair outside.

An attachment body

The more mutual presence of two bodies, two intersubjective bodies, with which I began this paper, was a moment that emerged out of the work with Peter over those two years. At the beginning, I do not think that he had a very developed sense of his own and other's subjective body. I think this lack was something that originated in his attachment experiences. He had developed a certain sort of fragmented attachment body. This "attachment body" is the body we develop through our interactions with our caregivers: the attachment ego is first and foremost an attachment body ego. As Susie Orbach (2009) puts it:

> … interpersonal, parental rearing relationships shape us from the outside and interpersonal, parental rearing relationships shape us from the inside, creating the specific architecture of our personal

brains. The behaviours create particular and personal neural pathways which affect and structure our biology in ways that are more explicit than any genetic predisposition. (Orbach, 2009, p. 140)

Peter is a white man from a working class background in his mid-forties. His father was a builder, now retired, and his mother, a part-time secretary. Peter was born with his disability, which meant that his legs did not develop properly, but that the rest of his body developed fairly normally. However, he had been able to walk for several years with the aid of calipers, before having to start using a wheelchair. It is unusual with Arthrogryposis for it to affect language and cognition, but Peter has been affected in this way—he has a stammer and stutters over first syllables of some words: especially words with high degrees of emotional content. His learning disability means he struggles to think—although I am not sure whether this difficulty thinking is necessarily related to his congenital disability, or a development that has arisen in relation to the traumas of his life, some of which I will describe shortly. I wonder about Peter's earliest affective body experience of his mother and father's responsiveness, and the impact of this on his developing sense of self. Pat Ogden (2006) has described the foundational role played by the early experience of an available and responsive embodied attachment figure:

> The social engagement system is initially built upon a series of face-to-face, body-to-body interactions with an attachment figure who regulates the child's autonomic and emotional arousal; it is further developed through attuned interactions with a primary caregiver who responds with motor and sensory contact to the infant's signals long before communication with words is possible. (Ogden, 2006, p. 42)

Services that support families whose children are born with, or develop, disabilities are not always adequate. The impact of having a child with special needs and then continuing to be their parent as they grow up is likely to be a profound, perhaps unsettling, experience and sometimes not unlike a form of chronic trauma. If the parents have, in addition, other unresolved relational traumas, these emotional-relational issues are likely to be further compounded. Describing such profound responses, Daniel Stern (1998) quotes a mother who has given birth to a child with a disability:

> I always imagined that one day I would be walking with my two children, holding each one by the hand. Now there is a gaping void in front of me. I don't know if I will have to spend my life taking care of an infant who could never walk. I don't know what will become of me. (Stern, 1998, p. 154)

Attachment theory has shown that intergenerational transmission can mean that the relational body patterns we develop are not just found and created in the relationship between carer and infant, they are also unconsciously passed on across the caregiving generations. When this "intergenerational body" holds significant unresolved trauma creating a sense of ontological wrongness, indications of disability may be very hard to bear. I think this may be what is being described by Bowlby (1969), referring to research on different forms of crying:

> A fourth type of crying given mainly by or only by infants with brain damage is reported to be especially disagreeable to the baby's companions who tend to become agitated and to wish to get out of earshot of it. (Bowlby, 1969, p. 290)

Peter began his psychotherapy with almost no conscious memories of his mother—or indeed very few memories about his family that he could express verbally. He was able to say that his mother had died when he was younger. Over time, he has gradually been able to say that she died from cancer when he was fifteen and to describe her being ill and his worry about her. With this have come memories of their relationship, especially their physical relationship together—about how much he felt like a small boy with her and used to long for her to cuddle him. Initially, not unusually perhaps, Peter idealised his mother, but as he spoke more of her, he remembered that he had been sent away as a boy to live in a mental handicap hospital for a number of years when he was a toddler, because his parents had been unable to cope. He remembers the experience of having to leave his parents and being in a cot, as a physical set of memories—remembering the smell, the lights, the feeling of being alone, struggling to stand up and holding the bars of the cot. He understands the reason for this was because he was disabled, because his body was different. This has been an ongoing difficult story of abandonment and profound grief for Peter.

A traumatised body

When we think about trauma with someone, inevitably we are bound to think about their relational body. This was true for Peter—I could not avoid it—and it was complicated by the issues associated with him also having a disabled body. His body seemed to evoke fear and hatred in others—a desire to attack it, and to be rid of it. His body, it would seem, can become a persecuting thing for the other, rather than being first and foremost an aspect of him as a person. Such fear and hatred—feelings any of us could feel—could be a response to being emotionally overwhelmed or frightened. The emotional experiences I have described here—both in the overwhelming mix of feelings and their intrinsically difficult nature, could generate further fear and then hatred in me. A fear of being further overwhelmed, not only by the significance to me of Peter's body difference; but also a fear and hatred communicated countertransferentially in both complementary and concordant forms (Racker, 1968). This is a countertransference experience that holds both the original parental emotional struggles with his disability, mixed up with Peter's own unformulated, unresolved trauma. These emotional experiences could unbalance me: the guilt, the feelings of intrusion and being relationally controlled, the unresolved grief in the parents, and the terror in Peter that comes with early abandonment. Feelings such as these can evoke both constrictive and intrusive responses in the psychotherapist. Powerful feelings like rage and hate can lie beneath such responses. Becoming conscious of these feelings, reflecting on and understanding them, are processes of particular importance in such work and mostly emerge through a good supervision relationship.

> The dialectic of trauma constantly challenges the therapist's emotional balance. The therapist, like the patient, may defend against overwhelming feelings by withdrawal or by impulsive, intrusive action. The most common forms of action are rescue attempts, boundary violations, or attempts to control the patient. The most common constrictive responses are doubting or denial of the patient's reality, dissociation or numbing, minimization or avoidance of the traumatic material, professional distancing or frank abandonment of the patient … The therapist should expect to lose her balance from time to time with such patients. She is not infallible. The guarantee of her integrity is not her omnipotence but her

> capacity to trust others. The work of recovery requires a secure and reliable support system for the therapist. (Herman, 1992, p. 151)

It has taken time to hear Peter's trauma stories. Firstly, these stories took time to tell because, like many traumatic memories, they were not held in a verbally formulated way in Peter's mind; but rather in fragments. Also, as with any trauma recovery, there was a need for security and regulation, for both the psychotherapist and the person, before the trauma-story could emerge and cohere sufficiently to be something that might then be explored.

There were two traumatic events that were connected in Peter's mind at least as attacks upon his body. One, when he was a young boy washing in the bath, and his mother was downstairs, his brother came into the bathroom and poured bleach down his back. He remembers, as he begins to tell me, the feeling of heat and burning on his back, and shouting. He remembers his brother laughing and then seeming to get scared. He remembers going under the water to get it off and then struggling to get out of the bath and his mum coming up. Through his remembering I see a registering of the trauma in his body, in an arching of his back, a shuddering and a holding himself with his arms. He could not remember what happened after his mother came up, nor what the consequences were for his relationships after this terrible attack. He still hated his brother, he thought he wanted to kill him. He sometimes thought it might have been better if he was killed at that time.

The second trauma, which Peter began to describe in the same session, so that the two events became quite mixed up in the telling, occurred a few years later in his life. His father left out some paint stripper in the house, on the "coffee table" he remembered. In fact he could describe the coffee table and the glass jar of paint stripper very well—like it was some sort of tantalising object. He picked up this jar of stuff and drank it and there was a burning in his throat and it was awful and he had to get himself outside and was shouting for help. He had to crawl round to the neighbour's house and was rushed to hospital. He nearly died he thought. Just like when he cut himself so badly across the chest with a kitchen knife he had to be rushed to hospital. There was a significant amount of rushing to hospital in Peter's life. In my mind I made connections with those experiences in his early life of being sent away to hospital. Judith Herman (1992) describes such self-attacks on the body as "perhaps the most spectacular of the pathological soothing mechanisms" (p. 109).

I did not want to believe any of these stories—experiencing "the countertransference press to disbelieve" (Dalenberg, 2007) like an attack upon my empathic connection with Peter. I did not want to believe that he could be so hated by a member of his family; nor did I want to believe that he could have taken this hatred into himself. With both of these stories it was easier for us to get to the fragmented painful drama of the event, but much more difficult to build a narrative of what happened relationally afterwards. The trauma had devastated Peter's memory of a repairing, caregiving relationship.

The hatred represented in his brother's act, and by several other attacks taking place in his adolescence, got inside Peter. A hatred that he did not experience in the fierce form of his own focused feeling, but as a "dysphoria":

> The normal regulation of emotional states is disrupted by traumatic experiences that repeatedly evoke terror, rage and grief. These emotions ultimately coalesce in a dreadful feeling called "dysphoria" that patients find almost impossible to describe. It is a state of confusion, agitation, emptiness and utter aloneness. In the words of one survivor, "Sometimes I feel like a dark bundle of confusion. But that's a step forward. At times I don't even know that much." (Herman, 1992, p. 108)

His wanting of my body was a way of trying to regulate himself out of this dysphoria: bringing himself into a desiring (not hating) relationship was a form of soothing.

These later traumas are a terrible addition to his earlier experiences of traumatic abandonment and loss. Perhaps the occurrence of these early traumas increased the likelihood of the later ones, especially as there was no opportunity for a healing working through. If an insecure attachment history does not always make later trauma more likely, it certainly does seem to make it more difficult to cope with. Peter's experience of separation at a young age and the loss of his mother at a time of key adolescent development were both about bodies. It was a separation that was predicated on the difference of his body from other bodies and on his parents being unable to cope with him, as he was with his body. The illness, which killed his mother, was a drawn-out withering attack on her body. As psychotherapists, we aim to understand traumatic repetition in relationships. We recognise how traumatic repetition occurs biopsychosocially across attachment spaces (Southgate, 1996). If there is no help with trauma, this repetition will inhabit and take control of the body.

A disabled body

Is the experience of a disabled body in itself an experience of trauma? Seeing how people with disabilities are treated in this civilised society in so many interactions, disability seems so often to lead to an experience of chronic abuse and neglect. The way in which a child with a disability is handled by the medical profession (themselves caught in a form of traumatised response), the lack of support for parents, carers, and other family members, the organisation of our disabling social environment and the engrained fear of physical wrongness can all be experienced as an ongoing grinding trauma by those involved. For Peter to live with his disability, in these different relational contexts, has been to live with a complex trauma. Sometimes it has been like living with ongoing abuse.

After about a year of working together, in which Peter and I were beginning to think together more about his experience and feelings about his disability (an area which was a long and ongoing conversation between us), Peter said he wanted to draw himself, to draw his body. He drew this picture:

This picture shocked me; it actually made me jolt back physically, like I was receiving a wave of powerful feeling. I was shocked by its vulnerability; in the splayed out flatness of the body—a body like a container into which something else has been inserted and left, or in which something else is living. A "something else" that is small and barely formed. It shocked me with its feeling of developmental earliness—that seemed so different from the verbal way Peter related to me. I was struck by the contrast between messy complexity (see the head area and the area in the middle) and minimalism and lacks (see the simple way the body is represented and the absence of hands). And it shocked me with its overwhelming significance—there seems to be so much present here.

> Missing or oversized facial parts represent a problem with reception of stimuli. Missing features indicate a denial of function, malfunction of the art(s), or a wish for less reception. If parts are enlarged, the disproportion reveals a bombardment or preoccupation with the function of those parts ... Missing hands or feet indicate a child's feeling helpless or immobile, unable to escape a situation. (Allen, 1988, p. 151)

Peter could not speak about his drawing for some time. I was aware of how much I could say about it, how much I could put inside. I wanted to talk about the baby inside, with perhaps another baby *mise en abyme* inside that—the small legs, the complicated and messy head, and the area at the centre. I was aware of a strong desire to re-enact something intrusive verbally and mentally, to do something relationally, which was a re-enactment of something that had occurred in relation to him with his body.

Over time we returned to this drawing of himself. Peter talked about having two bodies: about having the body he wants and having the body he has; the body he has with small legs. There was a complicated and messy head. Peter talked about how his brain did not work properly; how his feelings mean that his mind did not work properly. We had also at this time been talking about being a father and Peter's idea that he could never have had a child because of his disability, but feeling in himself the desire for a child.

The presence of bodies within bodies takes us to the thought that the multiple ego is first and foremost a multiple body-ego (Freud, 1923b). The work with Peter, like perhaps the work with everyone, is not just concerned with his body as a singularity, but with the presence of several different bodies. Here is a simple diagram of what I am exploring:

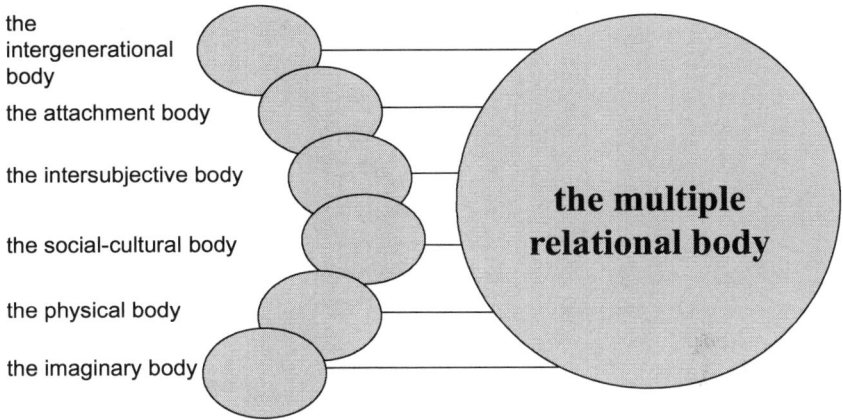

These are the bodies I find in psychotherapy.

- **The intergenerational body**—this is the body that is passed down to us through caregiving genetics—in the implicit relational domain across the generations.
- **The attachment body**—this is the body that we develop in our relationship with our immediate caregivers.
- **The intersubjective body**—this is the body that emerges mutually in the here and now relationship.
- **The social-cultural body**—this the body that we develop within in our social and cultural attachment space.
- **The physical body**—this is the material body, which grows, develops, gets ill, ages and dies.
- **The imaginary body**—this is the body we want, and the body we imagine we have, and maybe the body we do not want.

Trauma, with all its complex impact, may be present in relation to any one of these bodies. All of these bodies make a contribution to who we are, as a person with a multiple relational body. They may all appear in psychotherapy and probably they all need recognition and engagement from us. All of these different bodies can be alive (or dead) in the psychotherapy. Each person who comes to psychotherapy, together with the psychotherapist they meet, has their relationally made bodies, inhabited by an intergenerational history that is shaped by attachment securities, insecurities, and trauma. My mother's fear of physical closeness, and what is evoked in it, is embedded in me—shaping how I move, how I stand, how I sit and breathe, how I look and attend. My father is here in my body also. A more needing body; hurt by not being held. I look like my mother and father. And my mother and father come naturally with their own family histories. And the people themselves come with their own intergenerational body and attachment body. Together with this, arising out of these relational experiences, there are the imaginary bodies we have—those we love, hate, and desire, and the mutuality of intersubjective bodies. Then there is also our material physical body created by the internal and the external worlds. All of these bodies have a presence-absence, which is more or less apparent, dormant, or active, session to session, moment to moment, more or less conscious or unconscious.

Freud did not say the relational multiple ego is first and foremost a relational multiple body ego. I think the multiple relational nature of the body is experienced countertransferentially and unconsciously—this is the case more especially, and more powerfully, where there is such early ongoing trauma mixed together with an ongoing social and relational message of body wrongness. This became painfully apparent to me in my work with Peter, when in the midst of our conversations about his body and his disability and his desire for my body, I developed a painful swelling in my kneecaps. I struggled to walk and move about. Here I was being disabled:

> Most clinicians have probably had some experience of the uncanny, inexplicable and powerful resonances that can emerge between patient and analyst ... Whatever the substrate of such transmissions, they are certainly mutually constructed and often arise in treatments where there are complex sensitivities and vulnerabilities. (Harris, 1998, p. 41)

I felt guilty for my legs. I had daydreams about amputation—that the bursitis would become infected and I would be taken to hospital, in an emergency, to have them removed. Then I would sit with Peter, now identical—our painful difference removed, feeling more comfortable. Peter noticed how awkwardly I walked. I felt ashamed of this: that he had got into my body, visibly and undeniably. He wondered, in a doctor-like way, whether it was the cartilage that was a problem for me. The connective tissue was the area in which he thought I had pain and difficulty.

> Bodily countertransference experienced by the therapist has a very significant meaning in terms of the patient's unconscious communication of trauma: the client's own body communicates unbearable experiences not processed by the ordinary mechanisms of memory. (Lloyd, 2009, p. 74)

Conclusion

Something I can find awkward in my work with people with learning and physical disabilities is the fact that I do not have a disability—I am able-minded and able-bodied. Of course, I have times where my mind, brain and body do not work very well. I have also had experiences in my life that have put me in the position of being the outsider, and I can still struggle with an ongoing feeling of ontological wrongness. But these things are not the same as living with a learning and physical disability. This is for me a fact; sometimes a difficult fact that it is important to acknowledge as part of my work.

In conclusion at the conference, at the end of my paper, I showed a brief excerpt from a longer film called *The Examined Life* (2008), a documentary directed by Astra Taylor. The film features different philosophers walking around various cities, discussing the practical application of their ideas in modern culture. In the excerpt I showed, Sunaura Taylor, a woman with a similar disability to Peter, goes for a walk and talk with the philosopher Judith Butler. This excerpt can be seen on YouTube at the following link: www.youtube.com/watch?v=k0HZaPkF6qE.

I find this is a very moving piece of film. More than once I have cried when I have watched it. The film evokes powerful responses that inevitably involve our bodies. In their conversation and taking of a walk together, Taylor and Butler provide a social and relational understanding of the body that is a "challenge to individualism". For me, this political understanding has vital connections to attachment theory. Butler and Taylor make important links between the politics of disability and the politics of gender and, by implication, other areas of human difference. As Butler says, "A walk can be a dangerous thing". If we walk in the "wrong" sort of way there can be a hate-driven violent response to our difference. Peter has certainly experienced this in his relationships. Such hatred, like a post-traumatic response, is not that surprising in an environment that says there are certain things a proper body should be and do and others it should not be and do. Needing help from others, looking different, moving differently, can arouse strong feelings in us, which we may find especially difficult to manage if we have not had an experience of recognising caregiving. If we do have this somewhere in our lives, a walk together with someone different from us can become a creative experience.

Acknowledgements

I am very grateful to Peter for our walk together and for all that he has opened up and taught me in this psychotherapy. I also want to thank the students in the clinical seminar that I teach at The Bowlby Centre, who have heard about my work with Peter and given me their insights.

References

Allen, J. (1988). *Inscapes of the Child's World: Jungian Counselling in Schools and Clinics*. Putnam: Spring Publications.
Bowlby, J. (1969). *Attachment and Loss, Vol. 1. Attachment*. London: Hogarth Press and the Institute of Psycho-Analysis.
Dalenberg, C. (2000). *Countertransference and the Treatment of Trauma*. Washington: American Psychological Association.
Freud, S. (1923b). The Ego and the Id. *S. E.*, 19: 1–66. London: Hogarth.
Harris, A. (1998). Psychic envelopes and sonorous baths: siting the body in relational theory and clinical practice. In: L. Aron & F. S. Anderson (Eds.), *Relational Perspectives on the Body* (pp. 39–64). Hillsdale: The Analytic Press.
Herman, J. (1992). *Trauma and Recovery*. New York: Basic.
Lloyd, E. (2009). Speaking through the skin: the significance of shame. In: T. Cottis (Ed.), *Intellectual Disability, Trauma and Psychotherapy* (pp. 63–74). Hove: Routledge.
Ogden, P., Minton, K., & Pain, C. (2006). *Trauma and the Body*. New York: Norton.
Orbach, S. (2009). *Bodies*. London: Profile Books.
Racker, H. (1968). *Transference and Countertransference*. London: Hogarth Press and The Institute of Psycho-analysis.

Sinason, V. (1992). *Mental Handicap and The Human Condition*. London: Free Association Books.
Southgate, J. (1996). An attachment perspective on dissociation and multiplicity. A paper presented at The Third Annual John Bowlby Memorial Conference, 23 and 24 February 1996. London: Centre for Attachment-based Psychoanalytic Psycho-therapy (Incorporating the Institute of Self Analysis).
Stern, D. (1998). *The Birth of a Mother*. London: Bloomsbury.
Taylor, A. (2008). *The Examined Life*. Documentary film: www.youtube.com/watch?v=k0HZaPkF6qE [last accessed 5/09/2013].

APPENDIX ONE

Recommended reading

Anderson, F. S. (2008). *Bodies in Treatment: The Unspoken Dimension*. New York: Analytic Press.
Aron, L., & Anderson, F. S. (Eds.) (1998). *Relational Perspectives on the Body*. Hillsdale, NJ: The Analytic Press.
Boon, S., Steele, K., & Van der Hart, O. (2011). *Coping with Trauma-Related Dissociation: Skills Training for Patients and Therapists*. New York: Norton.
Brottman, M. (2011). *Phantoms of the Clinic: From Thought-Transference to Projective Identification*. London: Karnac.
Carroll, R. (2005). Rhythm, re-orientation and reversal: deep re-organisation of the self in psychotherapy. In: J. Ryan, (Ed.), *How Does Psychotherapy Work?* (pp. 85–112). London: Karnac.
Carroll, R. (2009). Self-regulation: an evolving concept at the heart of body psychotherapy. In: L. Hartley, *Contemporary Body Psychotherapy: The Chiron Approach* (pp. 89–105). Abingdon: Routledge.
Corrigall, J., Payne, H., & Wilkinson, H. (Eds.) (2006). *About a Body: Working with the Embodied Mind in Psychotherapy*. London: Routledge.
Cottis, T. (2009). *Intellectual Disability, Trauma and Psychotherapy*. London: Routledge.
Dalenberg, C. J. (2000). *Countertransference and the Treatment of Trauma*. Washington: American Psychological Association.

Eden, D., & Feinstein, D. (2008). *Energy Medicine: Balancing Your Body's Energies, for Optimum Health, Joy, and Vitality*. New York: Jeremy Tarcher.

Frank, R., & La Barre, F. (2011). *The First Year and the Rest of Your Life: Movement, Development & Therapeutic Change*. London: Routledge.

Galton, G. (2006). *Touch Papers: Dialogues on Touch in the Psychoanalytic Space*. London: Karnac.

Hartley, L. (Ed.) (2009). *Contemporary Body Psychotherapy: The Chiron Approach*. London: Routledge.

Hartung, J. C., & Galvin, M. D. (2003). *Energy Psychology and EMDR: Combining Forces to Optimize Treatment*. New York: Norton.

Herman, J. L. (1992). *Trauma and Recovery*. New York: Basic Books.

King, A. (2011). Touch as relational affirmation. *Attachment: New Directions in Psychotherapy and Relational Psychoanalysis*, 5: 108–124.

Klein, J. (1987). *Our Need for Others & Its Roots in Infancy*. London: Routledge.

Maroda, K. J. (2004). *The Power of Countertransference: Innovations in Analytic Technique*. London: Routledge.

Miller, A. (2011). *Healing the Unimaginable: Treating Ritual Abuse and Mind Control*. London: Karnac.

Mitchell, S. L. (2000). *Relationality: From Attachment to Intersubjectivity*. Hillsdale, NJ: Analytic Press.

Mollon, P. (2005). *EMDR and the Energy Therapies: Psychoanalytic Perspectives*. London: Karnac.

Mollon, P. (2008). *Psychoanalytic Energy Psychotherapy*. London: Karnac.

Montagu, A. (1987). *Touching: The Human Significance of the Skin*. New York: Harper Perennial.

Ogden, P. (2009). Emotion, mindfulness and movement: Expanding the regulatory boundaries of the window of tolerance. In: D. Fosha, D. Siegal, & M. Solomon (Eds.), *The Healing Power of Emotion: Perspectives from Affective Neuroscience and Clinical Practice* (pp. 204–231). New York: Norton.

Ogden, P. (2010). Modulation, mindfulness, and movement in the treatment of trauma-related depression. In: M. Kerman (Ed.), *Clinical Pearls of Wisdom: 21 Leading Therapists Offer Their Key Insights* (pp. 1–13). New York: Norton.

Ogden, P., & Fisher, J. (2009). Sensorimotor Psychotherapy. In: C. A. Courtois & J. D. Ford (Eds.), *Treating Complex Traumatic Stress Disorders, An Evidence Based Guide* (pp. 312–328). New York: Guilford Press.

Ogden, P., Minton, K., & Pain, C. (2006). *Trauma and the Body: A Sensorimotor Approach to Psychotherapy*. New York: Norton.

Ogden, P., Pain, C., & Fisher, J. (2006). A sensorimotor approach to the treatment of trauma and dissociation. *Psychiatric Clinics of North America*, 29: 263–279.

Orbach, S. (2004). The body in clinical practice, part one: there's no such thing as a body. In: K. White (Ed.), *Touch: Attachment and the Body* (pp. 17–34). London: Karnac.

Orbach, S. (2004). The body in clinical practice, part two: when touch comes to therapy. In: K. White (Ed.), *Touch: Attachment and the Body* (pp. 35–47). London: Karnac.

Orbach, S. (2009). *Bodies*. London: Profile Books.

Sinason, V. (2010). *Mental Handicap and the Human Condition*. London: Free Association Books.

Tiller, W. A. (2007). *Psychoenergetic Science*. New York: Pavior.

Totton, N. (2003). *Body Psychotherapy: An Introduction*. Maidenhead: Open University Press.

Totton, N. (2011). *Wild Therapy: Undomesticating Inner and Outer Worlds*. Ross-on-Wye: PCCS Books.

Totton, N., & Edmonson, E. (2009). *Reichian Growth Work: Melting the Blocks to Life and Love*. Ross-on-Wye: PCCS Books.

White, K. (2004). Touch: Attachment and the body. Introduction to the John Bowlby Memorial Conference 2003. In: K. White (Ed.), *Touch: Attachment and the Body* (pp. xxii–xxv). London: Karnac.

White, K. (Ed.) (2004). *Touch: Attachment and the Body*. London: Karnac.

APPENDIX TWO

The Bowlby Centre

Promoting attachment and inclusion

Since 1976 The Bowlby Centre (formerly known as CAPP) has developed as an organisation committed to the practice of attachment-based psychoanalytic psychotherapy. The Bowlby Centre is a dynamic, rapidly developing charity that aims both to train attachment-based psychoanalytic psychotherapists and to deliver a psychotherapy service to those who are most marginalised and frequently excluded from long-term psychotherapy.

We provide a four-year part-time psychotherapy training accredited by the UKCP and operate a psychotherapy referral service for the public, including the low-cost Blues Project. The Bowlby Centre has a wealth of experience in the fields of attachment and loss, and particular expertise in working with trauma and abuse. As part of our ongoing commitment to anti-discriminatory practice we offer a consultation service to the public and private sectors and are engaged in outreach and special projects, working with care leavers, women experiencing violence and abuse, offenders and ex-offenders, people struggling with addiction to drugs, alcohol, eating difficulties, or self harm, and to individuals and groups in a wide variety of mental health settings.

We run short courses on Attachment and Dissociation, and The Application of Attachment Theory to Clinical Issues, including learning disabilities. The Bowlby Centre organises conferences, including the annual John Bowlby Memorial Lecture, and has a series of publications that aim to further thinking and development in the field of attachment.

Bowlby Centre members participate extensively in all aspects of the field, making outstanding theoretical, research and clinical contributions. Their cutting-edge work is consistently published in the leading journals and monographs.

The Bowlby Centre values

- The Centre believes that mental distress has its origin in failed and inadequate attachment relationships in early life and is best treated in the context of a long-term human relationship.
- Attachment relationships are shaped in the real world and impacted upon by poverty, discrimination, and social inequality. The impact of the social world will be part of the therapy.
- Psychotherapy should be available to all, and from an attachment-based psychoanalytic perspective, especially those discriminated against or described as "unsuitable" for therapy.
- Psychotherapy should be provided with respect, warmth, openness, a readiness to interact and relate, and free from discrimination of any kind.
- Those who have been silenced about their experiences and survival strategies must have their reality acknowledged and not pathologised.
- The Bowlby Centre values inclusiveness, access, diversity, authenticity, and excellence. All participants in our organisation share the responsibility for anti-discriminatory practice in relation to race, ethnicity, gender, sexuality, age, (dis)ability, religion, class, educational and learning style.

Patrons
 Sir Richard Bowlby
 Dr Elaine Arnold

Trustees
    Janie Harvey-Douglas
    Prue Norton
    Jeremy Rutter
    Brian Ryerkirk

For more information please contact:
    The Bowlby Centre
    1 Highbury Crescent
    London N5 1RN
    020 7000 5070

Registered Charity, No. 1064780/0
Company Limited by Guarantee, N. 3272512

Email: admin@thebowlbycentre.org.uk
www.thebowlbycentre.org.uk

INDEX

Indexer: Dr Laurence Errington

Note: 'Freud' in subentries etc. refers to Sigmund Freud.

abuse (of children) 69, 102, 106, 116–117, 147
    clinical examples 94, 98, 104, 116–117, 119–120, 127, 135
    physical 98, 116, 119
    ritual 116
    sexual 6, 98, 116–117, 119, 127
acupuncture meridians 66–67, 72
adaptive responses to danger 92
advanced integrative therapy (AIT) 65
affect permeability or regulation (mode two) 14, 17, 19–25, 27–28, 30, 33–34
affective responses 21
    bodily based 49
agricultural society, sedentary, child-rearing 52–53
Ainsworth, Mary 4, 7
anticipatory movements 89, 99
applied kinesiology 72, 74
armouring 119
arousal levels 28, 102
    shifting 48
arthrogryposis 126, 130
Asheri, Shoshi 28–29, 34–36
Association for Comprehensive Energy Psychology 66
attachment xvii, 1–7, 24, 41, 52–54, 57, 79–80, 90–98, 101–103, 105
    avoidant 115

    Bowlby Centre's promotion of 148–149
    disorganised 53
    insecure xv, xvii, 53, 124
    secure 52, 54, 116
attachment body 129–131, 137–138
autism 56
autonomic nervous system 43, 47, 54
    see also parasympathetic nervous system; sympathetic nervous system
avoidant attachment 115

babies *see* infants and babies
Balint, M. 112, 114
Barker, Guy 52
beckoning action/gesture 100–101, 103
Bee (client) 119–121
Beebe, Beatrice 5, 19, 22, 89–90
behaviour
    non-verbal 95–96, 101, 105, 112
    transpersonal aspects of 74, 79–80
Benjamin, Jessica 31
bilateral stimulation 71
Bloom, Sandra L. 7
body, meaning 11–13
Boston Change Study Group 19, 48
Bowlby, John 2–4, 24, 91–93, 97, 99, 101–103, 105–106, 111, 125, 131

Bowlby Centre (formerly CAPP) xiv, xvii, 2, 4–5, 7, 147–149
   last know interview xviii–xix, 112–113
   see also John Bowlby Memorial Lectures
brain 89–90
   see also neuroscience
Bromberg, P. M. 23, 25, 29, 47, 93–95, 102–105

Callahan, Roger 71–73, 75–76, 85
Carroll, Roz xvi, 11–39
Cassidy, Jude 1, 7, 24
Centre for Attachment-based Psychoanalytic Psychotherapy (former name of Bowlby Centre) xiv, xvii, 2, 4–5, 7, 147–149
centring 56, 58
chakras 65–66, 68, 73, 78, 80, 84–85
Chiel and Beer 12
children
   abuse see abuse
   hyperactivity 79–80, 97
   infants and babies, procedural learning 90–91
   Neolithic changes in rearing 52–54
   special needs 130
   see also infants
Church, Hawk, Brooks, Toukolehto, Wren, Dinter, and Stein, energy psychology (2013) 69
Church, Piña, Reategui, and Brooks (2012), energy psychology 69
Church, Yount, and Brooks (2012), energy psychology 68
Claire (client) 114–116
clinical practice
   attachment and 6

countertransference xix
   examples xvii, 15–35, 98–106
   John Bowlby Memorial Lectures xiii, xv
   psychoanalytic energy psychotherapy 82–85
Connolly and Sakai (2011), energy psychology 68–69
consolidation touch 113
contact (Fritz Perls' use of term) 18
countertransference xiv, 5, 14, 16, 25, 47–49, 59, 79, 85, 110, 113–114, 117–118, 120, 122, 132, 134, 138
   bodily 139
cranial nerves 54–55

Damasio, Antonio 12, 20
danger (or its threat) 94, 97, 101, 103, 105
   adaptive responses to 92
   touch as 120
Davies, Jody Messler 5
decoding with self-states 94, 105
defensive responses 92, 96, 99
depression, mother 79–80
Diamond, John 66, 71–72, 74
disability xvii–xviii, 125–141
disorganised attachment 53
dissociation 21, 23–24, 29, 32, 36, 41, 95, 115, 118–119
DNA 66–67
drawing, Peter's 135–136

ego 54, 57, 70, 136, 138
   attachment body 129
   multiple 138
embodied relating
   outside therapeutic dyad xvi, 41, 43, 50–53, 59, 126
   therapeutic (embodied-relational therapy; ERT) 42, 51, 57–60

embodiment 12, 41–64
  intersubjectivity and 32
  thought 73
emotion and energy psychology 67, 70–74, 76–77, 79, 84–85
emotional body 77
emotional freedom techniques (EFT) 65, 71, 74
empty *vs.* full speech 45
enactment 26–29
encoding and self-states 94, 105
encounter (psychotherapeutic) xvi, 26, 54
energetic perception 18
  research evidence 68
energy field entrainment 80
energy psychology (EP) xvii, 42, 55, 66–74, 78, 83
  core principles and procedures 85
  information in the body and 71–74
  placebo effect and 75–76
  psychoanalytic energy psychotherapy (PEP) 80, 82–85
  randomised controlled trials 68–69
  subtle energy system 66–68, 71–72, 76, 78, 85
  transference and 81–82
engrams 47–49
  embodied-relational 47, 56
Epstein, Orit Badouk xiv–xv, xvii, 109–123
Esther (clinical example) 16–35
exaptation 55, 57
experience
  bodily 5, 16, 43, 45, 50
  of trauma (in the past), reliving 93–94

  see also self-experience
  transpersonal aspects of 74, 79–80
eye contact 17–18, 23, 31, 34, 55, 95, 98, 100, 119
eye movement desensitisation and reprocessing (EMDR) 70–71, 77

faces, exploration of 18–19
facing 56, 58
families wih disabled child, support services 130
Fang et al. (2009), energy psychology 68
feminism and intersubjectivity 32
fight or flight state/mode 55–56, 93, 99, 101, 120
film/video 19
Fonagy, Peter 5–6, 20
forager (hunter-gatherer) society 52–54
Freddie (client) 116–118
Freud, Sigmund 57, 69–72, 81–82, 112, 136, 138
full *vs.* empty speech 45

Gestalt theory and therapy 25–26, 32
Goodheart, George 65, 71–72, 74
grounding (and ground reference) 12, 36, 56
  touch and 113
guilt 117
  therapist's 127–129, 132, 138

hand tap, side of 75, 83
Harlow, Harry 111, 120
healing, obstacles to 74–76
heart 92, 102, 111
  social bonding and 54–56

Herman, Judith Herman 2, 6,
    133–134
holographic energy fields 66–67
homolateral energy flow 75
Hrdy, Sarah Blaffer 52–54
Hunter, Virginia xviii–xix, 112–113
hunter-gatherer (forager) society
    52–54
hyperactive children 79–80, 97

imagery 21, 26, 45, 54
imaginary body 137–138
imitation (babies) 42
impact (at bodily level) 49, 59
implicit relational knowing 15, 48,
    90–92
improvisation 20
inclusion, Bowlby Centre's
    promotion of 148–149
indirect touch 113–114
infants and babies
    affect regulation between parents
        and 22
    brain 90
    imitating others 42
    procedural learning 90
    separation from parents 2–3,
        111, 134
insecure attachment xv, xvii,
    53, 124
Intention Imprinted Electrical Device
    (IIED) 77–78
intentional movements 99
intergenerational body 131,
    137–138
internal state, perception 21
internal working models xv, 90–98,
    101, 103, 108
intersubjectivity (mode four)
    14, 32–35, 137
    embodied 60
intuition 15, 43–44, 113

Jenny (patient), psychoanalytic
    energy psychotherapy
    82–85
John Bowlby Centre (formerly
    CAPP) xiv, xvii, 2, 4–5, 7,
    147–149
John Bowlby Memorial Lectures
    1993–2011 xiii–xix, 1–7
    2012 (nineteenth) 7–8, 89–108
Johnson, Don Hanlon 58–59
Jones, Amanda 6–7
Judith Herman, Judith Herman 2–3,
    6, 133–134

Karatzias et al. (2011), energy
    psychology 69
Kepner, James 44–45, 50
kinesiology, applied 72, 74
Klein, Jo 5
Kurtz, R. 95–97

Lacan, Jacques 45
learning, procedural 90–91
Leary, Kimberlyn 5–6
libido 69–71
liminal awareness[::] 59
Linington, Mark xiv, xvii–xviii,
    125–141
loss, mourning of 4

Main, Mary 4, 6
Maroda, Karen 21, 49, 113
Mary (patient of Roger Callahan)
    72–73
meaning-making 24–25, 91
memory (memories) 26, 47, 131
    procedural 15–16, 47, 91
    recovery 51
    touch and 103, 109–117
    traumatic 116–117, 133
mental body 77
mentalization 5, 14, 24

meridians, acupuncture 66–67, 72
Miller, Alice 109, 115–116
mind, wild 42, 51, 74, 80, 83–84
mind–body energy system, different levels of 76–79
mindfulness 96–97
　clinical example 98–101
Miranda (client) 118–119
mirroring and mirror neurones 14, 20, 43, 49
Mitchell, Stephen 5
　modes 13–35
Mollon, Phil xvii, 65–88
Morrison, Tony 110–111, 122
mother
　depression 79–80
　Peter's (disabled child) 131
　sadistic 119–120
　see also parents
mourning of loss 4
movements (and actions)
　anticipatory 89, 99
　intentional 99
　repeated execution by infants/children 90–91
　Simon's (client) 94, 99–101, 103
multiple relational body 138–139
muscle testing 71–75, 79
　clinical example 82–84
mutual recognition 14, 31, 34

Neolithic changes in child-rearing 52–54
nervous system 16, 22
　autonomic see autonomic nervous system; parasympathetic nervous system; sympathetic nervous system
　see also cranial nerves; vagal nerve
neurological disorganisation 75

neuroscience 11–12, 14, 18, 20, 26, 41, 43, 54, 56, 60, 112
　see also brain
non-reflective behaviour (procedural organisation; mode one) 13–21, 23–24, 27–28, 30, 33
non-verbal behaviour 95–96, 101, 105, 112
nutrition in forager society, child 53

Ogden, Pat xv, 1, 7–8, 14, 18, 89–108, 130
one-body psychology 44
Orbach, Susie xiii–xiv, 5, 21, 25–26, 129–130
orgone 69–71

parasympathetic nervous system 43, 54–57
parents
　affect regulation between infant and 22
　separation from 2–3, 111, 134
　see also mother
Parkes, Colin Murray 1, 4
perception
　energetic 18
　of internal state 21
　of relational process 12, 15
Perls, Fritz 18
perspective-taking 24
perturbations (Callahan's) in psychoanalytic energy psychotherapy 85
Peter (disabled client) 126–139
phenomenology 18–19, 32
philosophy and intersubjectivity 32
physical abuse 98, 116, 119
physical body 14–15, 67, 77, 137–138
physics and energy pschology 77–79
placebo effect and energy psychology 75–76

polarity reversal 75
polyvagal theory 22, 54–57
postmodernism and intersubjectivity 32
post-traumatic stress disorder (PTSD) xvii–xviii, 1, 6, 69, 119, 140
preparatory movements 99
procedural learning 90–91
procedural memory 15–16, 47, 91
procedural organisation (mode one) 13–21, 23–24, 27–28, 30, 33
projections of others 26, 48, 79
projective identification 21, 79
proximity-seeking behaviour/ actions xv, 97–103, 106, 114
psychic energy 71
psychoanalytic energy psychotherapy (PEP) 80, 82–85
psychological reversal 75–76, 80, 83, 85

racism 5–6
reassuring touch 114
referral by disabled man (by himself) 129–130
reflexivity 15, 24–25, 36
Reich, Wilhelm 16, 42, 51, 69–71
relational body 131–132, 137
relational knowing, implicit 15, 48, 90–92
relational therapy/psychotherapy xiii, xv–xvii, 11–39, 50, 109
    embodied-relational therapy (ERT) 42, 51, 57–60
    relational body psychotherapy 42–44
relationships 42–43
    cranial nerves and interreelating 55
    embodied *see* embodied relating

psychotherapy on *see* relational therapy
somatising 44–50
therapeutic *see* therapeutic relationship
reorienting touch 113
rhythm 20, 44
ritual abuse 116

sadistic mother 119–120
Sanctuary Programmes 7
Schore, Alan 4–5, 21, 48–49, 91, 102
secure attachment 52, 54, 116
self-experience 45–46
self–other configuration (mode three) 14, 17–19, 23–31, 42
self-referral by disabled man 129–130
self-states 92–98, 103, 105
    clinical example (Simon) 101–102, 104, 106
    encoding and decoding with 94, 105
self-touch 103–104
Sella, Yorai 20, 24
semiotic speech 46
sensorimotor psychotherapy xv, 18, 97
separation from parents 2–3, 111, 134
sexual abuse 6, 98, 116–117, 119, 127
shame 27, 117, 121
    energy pathways and 84
shapes (being pushed or moved into or out of) 60
Sharpe, Ella 45
Siegel, D. 89
skin and touch 121
Slade, Arietta 6
social bond xvi, 41, 52–57
social engagement 43, 56–57, 95, 130, 135
socio-cultural body 137
somatising relationship 44–50

sounding 56
Southgate, John 2, 135
special needs child 130
speech 56
    embodied 45–46
    full *vs.* empty 45
Sperry, Roger 89
Stephen Porges, Stephen 22, 43, 54–57
Stern, Daniel 4, 45, 131
stomach meridian 72–73, 84
Strange Situation Procedure 4
subtle energy system 66–68, 71–72, 76, 78, 85
support services for families wih disabled child 130
sympathetic nervous system 43, 54–56, 92, 102

tapas acupressure technique (TAT) 65
tapping (acupoint) 65, 68, 70–71, 73, 75, 80, 83–84
telepathy 79
therapeutic relationship 14, 18, 34–35, 82
    bond in 109
    embodied-relational therapy (ERT) approach to 42, 51, 57–60
    mutual recognition in 14, 31, 34
    transference/countertransference *see* countertransference; transference
    unique choreography of each one 19–20
thought field and thought field therapy (TFT) 65, 73–74, 79–80, 85

threat *see* danger
Tiller, William 66, 71, 77–78
Totton, Nick xvi, 12, 14, 41–64
touch xviii, 15, 109–123
    in therapy 109–123
    memory and 103, 109, 116–117
    self 103–104
transference 5, 14, 25, 46–49, 57, 110, 117
    energy psychology and 81–82, 85
transpersonal aspects of human behaviour and experience 74, 79–80
trauma 5–6
    defensive responses with threat of 92, 96, 99
    disabled man (Peter) 132–135
    memory 116–117, 133
    reliving past experience 93–94
    therapies 70–71, 109–123
    see also abuse; post-traumatic stress disorder
Trevarthen, Colwyn xiv, 19, 42
two-body psychology 44, 126

vagal nerve 22, 54–55
van der Kolk, Bessel xvii
video/film 19
voice 56

White, Kate xiii–xix, 1–9
wild mind 42, 51
wild therapy 51
Winnicott, Donald xiv, 112
women, Neolithic changes in status 52–53
working models (internal) xv, 90–98, 101, 103, 108